T0274084

TALES OF LANCASTERS AND OTHER AIRCRAFT

GEORGE CULLING

TALES OF LANCASTERS AND OTHER AIRCRAFT

DANGEROUS SKIES
IN THE SECOND WORLD WAR

The History Press

I dedicate this book to former fellow members and friends of the Air Crew Association who are no longer with us, and hope that this modest volume will help to reassure their relatives and friends that they are not forgotten.

George Culling, Lancaster navigator 1944–45

First published 2017
Reprinted 2018
This paperback edition published 2023

The History Press
97 St George's Place, Cheltenham,
Gloucestershire, GL50 3QB
www.thehistorypress.co.uk

British Library Cataloguing in Publication Data.
A catalogue record for this book is available from the British Library.

ISBN 978 1 80399 455 0

Typesetting and origination by The History Press
Printed and bound in Great Britain by TJ Books Limited, Padstow, Cornwall.

MIX
Paper from
responsible sources
FSC® C013056

Trees for LYfe

CONTENTS

A Lancaster bomber during the royal fly past, June 2013. (Carfax2/Wikimedia Commons CC A-SA 3.0)

FOREWORD

The use of air power during the First World War became the subject of considerable analysis in the post-war era. Air commanders believed that the bomber would always get through and wars could be won by bombing alone. From the fall of France in 1940, the only way to hit back at Germany was to attack from the air. But it was soon realised that our aircraft lacked the necessary performance in range, bomb load and navigation at night with daylight raids suffering unsustainable high casualty rates.

Priority was given to the development of aircraft with long-range and large load-carrying capacity in parallel with electronic aids to navigation and target accuracy. The Halifax and Lancaster bombers equipped with Gee, Oboe and on-board H2S radar equipment became the mainstay of our attacks on Germany, and Bomber Command's sustained onslaught on strategic targets of the German war machine made a huge contribution towards bringing the war to an early end.

These raids were maintained on a daily basis regardless of the weather conditions or the losses suffered. For the aircrews it meant facing terrible hardships and casualties that were little known outside. Around 56,000 (just over 44 per cent) of the aircrew lost their lives. It was the highest loss rate of any other element of the armed forces, and more than the number of commissioned officers killed in the First World War. In addition, 8,000 were wounded and nearly 10,000 became prisoners of war.

George Culling trained as a navigator and flew numerous times in Lancaster bombers. He is able at first-hand to recount the stresses experienced by the crews – and some of their lighter moments – to provide a lasting record at a time when very few of his kind remain.

Alan Merriman
Air Vice-Marshal (RAF Retired)
CB CBE AFC* DL FRAeS

ACKNOWLEDGEMENTS

As always, I am grateful to my dear wife, Maureen, for all her support, encouragement and practical support.

Wings on the Whirlwind, a private publication, was the inspiration of the late John Guy, who worked tirelessly as Secretary of the North West Essex and East Hertfordshire branch of the Air Crew Association (ACA). My grateful thanks are due to Anne Grimshaw, the compiler and editor of that publication, who kindly gave me free rein to quote from it. I am also indebted to its contributors, all of whom were branch members. Some of their stories point to incredibly brave actions, many of which are very moving, and their achievements, and those of other aircrews, should be more widely known.

I am also grateful to Alan Merriman, Air Vice-Marshal (RAF Retired) CB CBE AFC*DL FRAeS, who was our branch president and who kindly wrote the foreword.

John Gerrard has been very helpful in several ways, including the provision of photographs, and Barry Wiseman and Stephen (C) have always been willing to help me with computer problems and the placing and arrangement of photographs within the text.

I much appreciated the generous help provided by the prolific author Michael Bowyer, who scanned my text and offered some useful suggestions.

I have been fortunate to have the encouragement and support of Amy Rigg and her colleagues from The History Press.

This book would have never seen the light of day without contributions from the aforementioned and I feel very lucky to have had such help. Obviously I take complete responsibility for all the facts and opinions expressed, and all errors of omission and commission.

INTRODUCTION

Tales of Lancasters and Other Aircraft records a wide range of unexpected – and often extremely unwelcome – events occurring, mainly in the air, during the Second World War. Some led to death or injury; some were simply a nuisance; others were bizarre, and even hilarious, especially in retrospect.

It is not always appreciated that wartime airmen faced a variety of potentially hazardous situations apart from when they were called upon to face the enemy. Fortunately, not all of the happenings described here resulted in casualties – though many did (see Chapter 1) – but they were seen as perhaps an inevitable part of an airmen's life in wartime.

Some of this book is about my own experiences as a navigator – in training during the Second World War, between 1944 and 1945, while flying in an Anson, a Wellington and a Lancaster. In the Lancaster, I first used radar aids – H2S and Gee – but with the ending of the European war, I navigated our Lancaster using only the stars as a navigational aid. This was in preparation for the Pacific War and continued right up to the dropping of atom bombs on Japan. In that period I certainly had some rather eerie experiences, which I have described.

Altogether, however, the book presents, I believe, a rounded picture of the typical hazards faced by wartime airmen, particularly those who flew on operations over enemy territory, of whom 44 per cent – over 56,000 – perished. They included pilots, navigators (at one time called 'observers'), bomb aimers, wireless operators, flight engineers and gunners, and those such as wireless operator/gunners, who performed more than one role in their crew. And they ranged in age from a Canadian of 16, who died a few weeks before the end of the war, to some who were over 50, though the average was about 22.

★ ★ ★

Main view of the pilot area of the Avro Lancaster B Mk I at Paine Field, USA, in 2010. (John Veit/Wikimedia Commons CC0 1.0)

Many years after the Second World War, Anne Grimshaw, editor of *Wings on the Whirlwind*, wrote in her introduction about the difficulty of getting ex-aircrew to talk about their experiences:

> There is no 'line-shooting', no bragging, no derring-do, no heroics; indeed, many men were often casual and dismissive of what they did, and it was sometimes difficult to get them to tell me what they did that could be considered 'brave'.

They hadn't changed. Like other servicemen, RAF airmen usually discouraged the slightest sign of boasting. Shooting a line was no route to popularity. Laughing at absurdities was more appreciated.

Nor was it 'the done thing' to discuss the loss of friends at any length, sad news being communicated between airmen, perhaps as: 'I'm afraid poor old Bill, Nobby and Tom "went for a burton" over Hamburg last night.' Or perhaps: 'Freddy and Jim got the chop attacking those marshalling yards near Berlin.'

One aircrew member might say to another who was about to prepare for an op, 'If you get the chop tonight, can I have your bike?' or some other article he had pretended to covet. And such an apparently appalling and insensitive remark would occasion plenty of laughter all round, in which the airman about to fly would fully share. Such humour helped to maintain a veneer of cheerfulness and helped to sublimate inner tensions.

The official motto of the RAF is '*Per Ardua ad Astra*' (Through Struggle to the Stars). It was adopted in 1912 by the Royal Flying Corps (the forerunner of the Royal Air Force, which was created in 1918). Somewhat less elegant but equally meaningful, during the Second World War, was the popular 'Press on Regardless'. The airmen whose stories I have recorded certainly did that.

THE AIR CREW ASSOCIATION

The Air Crew Association (ACA), with branches all over Britain and the Commonwealth, was formed with a membership mainly of aircrew from the Second World War to foster comradeship among all those awarded an official flying badge to operate aircraft in the service of Britain, the Commonwealth and the Allies.

Perhaps surprisingly, it was not formed until 1977, thirty-two years after the ending of that war, when its members had raised their families (some had even become grandparents) and were fully established in their chosen careers, or had retired.

Inevitably, the vast majority of them had, by 2011, passed away, and in that year the central organisation was dissolved, leaving branches to continue informally where that was possible.

The North West Essex and East Hertfordshire branch of the ACA, of which I was a member, had to close but a small group of us continues to meet as an ACA luncheon club.

The ACA Archive Trust seeks to preserve key aircrew memorabilia contributed by members and their beneficiaries.

1

AN OVERVIEW OF SOME OF THE EXPERIENCES OF RAF AIRCREWS IN THE SECOND WORLD WAR

There were many serious accidents during the training of aircrews. Many were related to inexperience, some were caused by seriously bad weather conditions, several resulted from instrumental failure and others were attributed to a variety of other causes. Altogether over 8,000 were killed in training accidents and other non-operational flying (Air Ministry).

Those casualties should be considered alongside the chilling statistic of a death rate of about 44 per cent (see Introduction) relating to operational crews. At one time, half of the crews were lost before they had completed ten operations and fewer than one in eight airmen survived fifty operations. The life expectancy of crews was particularly short between March 1943 and May 1944, when the chances of surviving a tour of thirty operations were considered about one in five. Many aircrews had to bail out of their damaged aircraft, and well over 9,000 of them became prisoners of war (POWs).

In 1943, at the age of 18, eighty years ago, I joined the RAF in the PNB (pilot, navigator, bomb aimer) category, whose members would train together for over three months. During the very first week, a drill sergeant told us that we might have about eighteen months to live, whereas air gunners should expect no longer than six months.

In Kevin Wilson's *Men of Air* he quotes an airman who arrived at an operational station to be told by the intelligence officer: 'Your expectation of life is six weeks. Go back to your huts and make out your will.'

It would seem that aircrews, even in training, were not allowed to nurse any delusions, but few were worried by these sardonic predictions, whilst appreciating that they contained more than a grain of truth.

★ ★ ★

It wasn't only enemy anti-aircraft fire and night fighters that posed a threat to crews attacking at night. Weather could be a particular problem. Very cold air temperatures might cause a build-up of ice, up to 6in deep, on the wings of an aircraft, thereby seriously affecting its lift. Engines or wireless sets could freeze up and stop working altogether. Electrical storms could affect the compass or cause a fire. 10/10ths cloud (complete cloud cover) often made map reading impossible when other navigational aids were not available or unserviceable.

An aircraft forced to land in thick fog was always in danger. The pilot would descend tentatively and blindly through the swirling fog, searching desperately for familiar features, always with one eye on his altimeter – an instrument with varying degrees of accuracy. The aircraft might crash at any time, into a hill, a hangar, an electric cable or some other obstruction. Many did.

Instruments sometimes failed. An Air Speed Indicator (ASI), for example, might fail during take-off, causing an overshoot of the runway.

The oxygen system or the heating system might fail. Both, at different times, became unserviceable while I navigated a Lancaster, the latter creating polar conditions (see Chapters 6 and 7).

Then there were accidents, sometimes, but not always, the result of human error.

A young pilot in training, used to handling lighter aircraft, and landing a Lancaster at a Heavy Conversion Unit (HCU), perhaps for the first time, might overshoot, or run out of runway, through his lack of familiarity with heavy, four-engine aircraft. Or a tyre might burst or the flaps might not work when landing.

Aircraft returning from operations were often so badly damaged that landing could be extremely hazardous. Or pilots might have to land with their full bomb load because the bomb mechanism jammed at the critical moment on the bombing run.

If they had to land with a damaged aircraft *and* a full bomb load, the landing could be extremely dangerous, and even the most highly skilled pilots might well not be able to avoid a calamitous explosion.

When several aircraft had returned from an operation and were awaiting instructions to land, their priority had to be decided with some urgency. There were three main considerations: the aviation fuel reserves, the presence of wounded aircrew members – and the severity of the injuries – and the damage to the aircraft.

There were sometimes accidents during close formation flying, especially of heavy bombers when, for example, one of them might be caught in the slipstream of another, causing both to crash.

Aircraft attacking at night and near the target area often 'corkscrewed' away from searchlight cones and anti-aircraft fire. With other aircraft also taking evasive action, collisions were a constant danger. There could be scores of aircraft in the target area, some intent on completing their bombing run with straight and level flight, so there was also the risk that one aircraft might drop bombs on another. There were several cases of that occurring, more than one aircraft returning to its base with a bomb hole in one of its wings, the bomb having fortunately passed right through without exploding.

Fatigued pilots returning from night operations sometimes forgot to lower their undercarriages before landing, so that the belly of the fuselage scraped along the runway, out of control. If it then skidded off the runway, it might crash into a parked aircraft, a petrol bowser or something else.

Low-level bombing of enemy shipping was always dangerous. Apart from the flak from a ship's anti-aircraft guns, a very low-level attack to ensure accuracy might result in the aircraft being caught in the bomb's explosion. One such attack was so low level that the attacking aircraft returned with part of a ship's mast sticking out of it.

Examples of many of the above happenings are recorded in Chapter 10. They were described by members of the North West Essex and East Hertfordshire branch of the ACA.

There are two such events to which I have given special attention in Chapters 11 and 12 – one is about the navigator of a Mosquito aircraft, who at 28,000ft managed to roll off the wing of his blazing, doomed aircraft, in order to get clear of the aircraft before operating his parachute. The other features an air gunner, wounded by shrapnel, who also managed to bail out of a blazing aircraft – a Stirling.

He became a POW, and was later caught up in the miserable march undertaken by POWs towards the end of the war. It's a story that moves me every time I read it.

I thought the experiences of Gerry Carver were remarkable and also merited a separate chapter.

I was very pleased to hear about Cliff Storr and his experience as a navigator on about fifty operations, and he too has a separate chapter.

★ ★ ★

In other parts of this book there are two accounts of almost unbelievably brave actions, both of which led to the award of the Victoria Cross (VC).

The first (page 52) is about Sergeant James Ward, who climbed out of his Wellington aircraft, made holes in the wing for hand and foot holds, and, buffeted by the slipstream, worked his way along the wing, towards a blazing fire in one engine. He succeeded in smothering the flames, saving the aircraft and the lives of all the crew.

The second (page 164) is even more incredible. Sergeant Norman Jackson, though injured by shrapnel from anti-aircraft guns, climbed out on to the wing of his aircraft in order to put out an engine fire. A fighter-bomber then attacked and two bullets hit him in the leg. His eyes and hands were burned but he succeeded in smothering the flames before being swept away in the slipstream.

Altogether there were about twenty VCs awarded to members of RAF bomber crews.

★ ★ ★

In the early years of the war, Blenheim and Whitley aircraft carried the main burden of the leaflet dropping and bombing campaign (see Appendix for descriptions and photographs of the bombers we had in 1939).

The following is one event from those days – a fluke – that ended happily. During a pamphlet raid on 27–28 October 1939 by Whitley bombers, one was very severely damaged by enemy fire and made a particularly heavy crash landing in a field in France. The rear gunner was badly shaken up. He went to have a word with the pilot and discovered to his amazement that he was alone. Everyone else had bailed out but he had not heard the order owing to a breakdown of the intercom. The aircraft had made the landing without anyone at the controls. The rear gunner was fully aware of how close he must have been to death. But where were his fellow crew members?

Still very dazed, he walked to a nearby village, where, to his relief, he found the rest of the crew in a café, and learnt what had happened to them. They were astonished both to see him and to hear that their aircraft had not actually crashed even though it was far too badly damaged ever to fly again.

And how had they fared? The front gunner had been knocked unconscious by his parachute when it opened. He opened his eyes to find himself in a field, surrounded by curious but friendly cows. The wireless operator landed in a field full of hostile bulls and had to sprint towards a hedge in full flying kit. The navigator sprained an ankle. The captain landed softly and was unhurt. All were given bouquets by the French and taken to a hospital for treatment.[1]

NOTES

1 *Bomber Command*, page 33

2

WAS MY PILOT TRAINER 'ROUND THE BEND'?

They can fly upside down with their feet in the air,
They don't think of danger, they really don't care.
Newton would think he had made a mistake,
To see those young men and the chances they take.

Extract from song in the film *Those Magnificent
Men in their Flying Machines*

★ ★ ★

The Tiger Moth is a two-seater (one seat being behind the other) propeller-driven biplane, designed by Geoffrey de Havilland, and has been flown since the early 1930s. Mainly used as a primary trainer, it followed de Havilland's earlier Gypsy Moth, the aircraft in which Amy Johnson flew solo to Australia in 1930. For pilot training it had dual control.

It has to be started by hand by someone giving the propeller a firm turn. That has to be executed with some skill: otherwise a propeller that suddenly bursts into rapid movement as the engine splutters into life could easily strike the turner. It can take off and land on any reasonable meadow.

For learner pilots, it's fortunate that the Tiger Moth is robust, so that it tolerates inexpert handling quite well, as I can attest.

* * *

It was 1944. To determine my suitability as a pilot – for my own sake as well as the RAF's, I opted to have up to ten hours of instruction in a Tiger Moth. I really wanted to become a navigator but the opportunity to have free flying lessons in an open cockpit was too good to miss.

Sadly, my piloting efforts, quite promising at first, ended rather disastrously but I'm glad I accepted the opportunity. The whole experience was quite unforgettable, and not only for the obvious reasons.

A propeller-driven Tiger Moth biplane. Throughout the Second World War, RAF airmen recruited for the PNB category might be given up to ten hours' pilot training to test whether they had the aptitude for it. Many flew solo well within that period. (Łukasz Golowanow & Maciej Hypś/Konflikty.pl/Wikimedia Commons)

I met my pilot instructor near the aircraft. He was an unbelievably odd looking little fellow and I'm afraid I saw him as a tadpole in an officer's uniform. Fronting his large, shiny, bald head, he sported a huge, black, waxy, handlebar moustache in the finest RAF tradition, which tapered to fine points and wobbled precariously above his lips, especially when he spoke, when its wavering had an almost hypnotic effect. He reminded me of Pilot Officer Prune featured in the training magazine *Tee Emm* (Training Memorandum), who constantly pranged his aircraft through foolish misdemeanours in each issue. The humorous, cartoon approach to putting across valuable flying lessons was very effective and may well have prevented many accidents, and saved many lives.

However, he was a flying officer, an 'old man' of about 25, while I was an 18-year-old sprog airman. Besides, I would very soon be utterly dependent on him, and I did appreciate that he might well be an excellent pilot and instructor.

These would not be simply my first flying lessons. I had never before had an opportunity to fly, even as a passenger. Now, I would have a wonderful opportunity to get a bird's eye view of the world from an open cockpit. It should be an experience to savour for years afterwards; it was.

I certainly enjoyed the first few lessons. It was wonderful to look below at the beautiful English countryside and flying straight and level, banking to turn, climbing or descending, posed no problems.

Away from built-up areas and at a reasonable height, say, 5,000ft, we could carry out a spin. The instructor told me to pull the control column gently backwards until the plane slowed and was just hovering and about to stall. That was the precise moment when I should push out one foot or the other to operate the left or right rudder pedal and then we would go into a spin. And so we did. That was an exhilarating experience. I looked down and the world below of green fields, hedgerows and trees, was spinning rapidly around the nose of the aircraft as it hurtled towards the ground, apparently out of control.

Watching fascinated, while the rotating countryside came ever closer, I then pushed out my foot to operate the pedal I had not used previously, and opened the throttle fully.

With a great roar, we pulled out of the spin and soon climbed back to our former height, where straight and level flight could be resumed.

My take-offs were probably not perfect but this is again a relatively simple operation in a Tiger Moth. As we ran over the grass I opened the throttle, at first moving the control column a little forward to keep the aircraft on its two front (pram) wheels, with the tail wheel in the air. Then with a good speed having been established, I gently pulled back the control column to lower the tail plane. The Tiger Moth then soared smoothly into the sky and I climbed to the height required by my trainer.

My landings were more problematical, some being much less error-strewn than others. I had to take a good look at the wind sock to determine the right direction of approach, to land against the wind; and then descend very carefully so that I might achieve something like a three-point landing on the grass, which I managed on only about half of my attempts.

However, I believe that, up to that point, my instructor was reasonably satisfied with my progress.

And then, quite suddenly, he wasn't! During my fourth lesson, and without warning, I became quite deaf. I was immediately cut off from all communication, and felt quite alone and isolated in my silent world. The changes in air pressure, combined with some lively manoeuvres had brought about my absolute deafness. I was naturally dismayed and very embarrassed, but there was obviously nothing that I could do about it.

The reaction of my flying instructor was not in the least bit sympathetic to my predicament. He cursed and shouted so loudly that some of his vituperation and colourful language actually reached me in a garbled sort of way. I realised that he was not only frustrated, which was to be expected, but also beside himself with fury, when he began to move the wings violently up and down as if trying to arrest my attention.

He kept up those ineffectual wing movements for several minutes; then he began to move the aircraft about furiously, at one time flying it upside down.

When he did that, I felt my whole body suddenly, and alarmingly, shift position, to leave me no longer sitting firmly on my seat but hanging helplessly by my straps. I remember wishing that I had been warned of that manoeuvre before take-off so that I could have checked that my straps were as tight as possible. As it was, I felt anything but secure with my head dangling some thousands of feet above the countryside.

Then more unexpected and often very violent movements of the aircraft took place until my instructor, apparently having fully expressed his anger and frustration, dipped the nose of our Tiger Moth, carried out a rapid descent, and, somewhat to my relief, brought it down to land.

In spite of his idiosyncratic manoeuvres in the air, which convinced me that he was round the bend, I was ready to apologise to my instructor and explain what had happened to me in more detail.

Sadly, there was no opportunity. Once we had both descended from our cockpits, he confronted me, red faced, with an expression contorted with fury. I can't remember everything he said as once again his absurd moustache wobbled about uncontrollably while his words spilled out, completely undermining their content. He then stormed away, leaving me with no opportunity to say anything, and that was the last I ever saw of him.

I had now reached a clear decision. I had enjoyed my flying lessons except for the last one but that had ended so miserably that I was now determined to become a navigator. I therefore lost no time in informing my commanding officer that I wished to have no more flying lessons.

I was then required to take some aptitude tests for would-be navigators, which included matching dozens of aerial photographs of urban and rural areas with ordnance survey maps at speed. I found that a most interesting challenge and raced through the test with enjoyment.

A few days later, I joined a long queue of PNB airmen, all anxious to know whether they were destined to become pilots, navigators, bomb aimers or gunners. The latter possibility was a new and disturbing development, and added to our apprehensions as we shuffled forward in the queue.

We had been told that the RAF had lost so many gunners – mostly rear gunners – that a proportion of PNBs would be required to remuster and boost their number. We all knew that the casualty rate among gunners was very high; enemy fighters usually attacked the tail of a bomber to put the rear gunner out of action before focusing on other vulnerable parts of the aircraft (see Chapter 17).

Although we were fully prepared to face the inevitable hazards of being members of aircrews, few of us wanted to be gunners. It wasn't simply a matter of degrees of danger. We had all enlisted as PNBs, and that was where our interests were. The would-be pilots, especially, were passionately keen to fly and skipper an aircraft. They had volunteered precisely with that in mind.

Finally I reached the head of the queue and I was soon face to face with a wing commander, who appeared to be constantly frowning while he spent a few minutes examining my records. My doubts and concerns increased. What would be my fate?

Then he looked up, his expression just as serious as when I entered the room, so that I had no clue about what to expect. I was rather tense and told myself to prepare for the worst.

He then quietly announced that I would be accepted for training as a navigator. I was absolutely delighted, and the wing commander, noting my unalloyed pleasure, metamorphosed into a friendly companion, shook my hand warmly and wished me well.

Wonderful. The sun was shining. All was well with the world. I left him in a dream.

Looking back, although my first navigation exercise was less than satisfactory, for reasons beyond my control, I really enjoyed navigating. It was always challenging and full of interest. To fix the aircraft's position at regular intervals, to calculate the speed and direction of the wind and based on that to produce a course for the pilot to steer that would keep the aircraft on track, was a creative task that I found deeply satisfying. And later, when I navigated a Lancaster using only the stars as a navigational aid, it was even better.

So perhaps my wacky Pilot Officer Prune actually did me a good turn.

3

LOST OVER
THE IRISH SEA

HOW A SPROG NAVIGATOR NAVIGATED AN ANSON AIRCRAFT TO THE WRONG CITY

The Avro Anson had its maiden flight in December 1935, and served the RAF until 1968. It was a low-wing monoplane with two radial engines (cylinders arranged in a circle). If one engine failed in flight, it was difficult for the aircraft to remain airborne.

The wings were made of plywood and spruce and the fuselage of steel tubes covered in fabric and plywood.

At one time it was fitted with a dorsal gun turret for the use of Coastal Command and intended for marine reconnaissance and search and rescue.

However, the Anson was used much more for the training of navigators, bomb aimers, wireless operators and pilots. The original dorsal turret with its machine gun was then removed, except of course when the aircraft was used for training air gunners.

Avro Anson 652A Mk I (Reg. ZK-RRA, S/No. MH-120) at Ardmore Aerodrome de Havilland Mosquito Launch Spectacular, 2012. (L-Bit/Wikimedia Commons CC A-SA 3.0)

It has many square windows – hence its nickname 'the Flying Greenhouse' – which made it excellent for navigational training. It was also known, because of its relatively long life, as 'Faithful Annie'.

Its undercarriage was retractable, but had to be wound up by turning a handle at least 147 times – a very tedious task. Sometimes pilots with no one aboard to do the donkey work left the undercarriage down, which reduced speed by about 30 knots. A warning horn sounded when that happened but frustrated pilots sometimes disconnected it. This was the very first retractable landing gear in the RAF. The one pictured above was with the RCAF.

Pilot: 'I'm still flying on the first course you gave me, navigator; the one you provided before take-off. Have you worked out a new one yet?'

Me: 'I'm afraid not, sir. I want to get some compass bearings but all the headlands and islands we're flying over are covered in cloud. I can't see anything that I can use for getting a bearing. Below us, there's stratus cloud everywhere.'

Pilot: 'Yes, I can see that. Have you tried to get a radio bearing?'

Me: 'Yes, sir, but the wireless operator says the radio has just gone kaput.'

Pilot: 'So what are you going to do?'

Me: 'I wondered whether you could descend to just below cloud level for a few minutes, sir. I'm sure we're flying near the coast, where there are plenty of headlands and rocks that I can use. I'll then be able to fix our position very quickly, and calculate a new course in a jiffy.'

Pilot: 'Not a chance, navigator. I'm sure we're flying near the coast, but I'm not going to take any risks to make your life easier. Have you anything else in mind?'

Me: 'At the moment, no, sir.'

Pilot: 'Then we'll just have to assume that we're on the way to Fishguard, won't we? And like Mr Micawber, we'll have to hope that something turns up.'

And, in fact, something did turn up.

* * *

I had expected to be sent for training to what I saw as one of the more glamorous, and drier, parts of the world – Rhodesia (as it was), Arizona or Canada – the destination of most other trainee navigators. What happened to me would never have occurred, for instance, over the sunny plains of Alberta.

I'd groaned when I heard about my posting. I knew nothing about the Isle of Man, except that it was being used for the internment of people thought to pose some risk to Britain's security. (In fact, the vast majority of internees, I'm sure, were loyal, patriotic citizens who happened to have Germanic names. War makes some unfair decisions inevitable.)

With about twenty other trainee navigators, I was stationed at an RAF aerodrome at the very north of the island – Jurby, near the Point of Ayr.

Scotland's Mull of Galloway, a long, fat, pointing finger of land, was visible to the north-east, and the massive St Bees Head, westernmost point of the Lake District, to the east. The Mountains of Mourne in Northern Ireland could be seen to the west, on a fine day.

Jurby would be our home for the next six months, in Nissen huts, which consisted of long, semicircular, corrugated-iron slabs, fixed to a concrete floor. During the winter, the stove in the centre roasted airmen within a few yards, while almost everyone else was freezing cold.

On navigational exercises, we would fly in an Anson aircraft. We would be navigating for about six months to every part of the Irish Sea, up to Scotland's Outer Hebrides, and at the end of that period I hoped to be a qualified navigator.

To fix our position at regular intervals we would need to take three compass bearings of salient features such as Ailsa Craig, St Bees Head, and the Mull of Galloway. Or we could equally well fix it by taking bearings of the same object at various time intervals.

Each bearing would enable us to plot a 'position line', (somewhere along which we were travelling) on a Mercator chart. Three 'position lines' (two having been transferred to equalise the times) would (we hoped) intersect to fix our position.

We then had to compare our fixed position to where we would have been if there was no wind (on an air plot of courses steered) in order to calculate the wind speed and direction. We would then use that to work out a new course to give to the pilot.

Finally, the day arrived when I would have my first opportunity to navigate an aircraft – an exciting prospect. I'd be able to put into practice all those procedures that had featured in the navigation theory I had studied for many months.

I was 18, and full of optimism.

But overshadowing my thoughts was the intimidating presence at the station of Flight Lieutenant Biss, responsible for assessing all charts and logbooks after every flight. Biss was as unpopular as he was unpleasant, with almost everyone, and on our return we would all, in turn, have to confront him, to hear his verdict on our efforts. If the slightest thing were to go wrong, he would come down on us like a ton of bricks – or so everyone said.

However, I was reasonably confident that nothing would go wrong. I'd thought of everything – or so I thought – and planned the flight with meticulous care.

In the event, however, my first navigation exercise was hardly the triumph I had envisaged because there was one aspect that was absolutely out of my control – the weather.

Until I heard the dismal forecast at the Met briefing, of 10/10ths stratus cloud (complete coverage of grey cloud), I was on top of the world. On the way to the aircraft, however, I had much to think about. How many landmarks would I actually see on a drizzly, grey day such as this? Perhaps there would sometimes be breaks in the cloud enabling me to take some bearings? I had to hope.

In the air, we novice navigators worked in pairs, taking turns to do the real work, the 'second navigator' playing second fiddle by winding up the undercarriage and occasionally map reading. We had to plot every detail of our work on the chart, including courses steered, track (path over the earth's surface) and wind velocity, and also keep a log of every activity we carried out. Flight Lieutenant Biss, we were told, would expect the highest standards – or else …

I made sure that I had everything I needed including an Omega watch, chart, logbook, 2H and 3H pencils (sharpened like chisels), a ruler, compasses and a square protractor, and I worked out my flight plan with provisional courses to give to the pilot, for each leg, based on forecast wind velocities.

It went wrong almost from the start, and there seemed nothing that I could do to save the situation.

The Met forecast was accurate: there was stratus cloud everywhere – a sheet of grey cloud with a base of about 2,500ft, which completely screened the earth's surface from view. A depressing sight and a miserable baptism for a fledgling navigator.

I gave the pilot a course for Fishguard, in Pembrokeshire. He decided to fly at about 3,500ft. Aircraft should always fly at an altitude of at least 1,000ft above any mountains within 20 miles of our proposed track. We had to take into account the various Scottish and Welsh mountains, the fells of the Lake District and the Mountains of Mourne in Northern Ireland.

Hopefully, we were a safe distance from all of them, but we couldn't be absolutely sure until I had fixed our position – and that proved to be an intractable problem.

All I could see in every direction below our aircraft was a monotonous grey carpet, which completely screened the world from view. Somewhere below that carpet was a wonderful coastline of bays, estuaries, islands and headlands. So compass bearings, which were our priority, were out of the question.

I was therefore absolutely dependent on radio bearings – my only hope of saving the situation. So I spoke to the wireless operator, requesting a bearing. After a few minutes he contacted me to give me the bad news. The radio had suddenly given up. It was absolutely dead and there was apparently little prospect of any improvement. 'My God,' I thought, 'what's next?'

During this training stage we had no access to radar, and there was no other resource open to me, for the time being anyway. Had it been a night flight I would have used the stars. I had to fall back on my flight plan, based on forecast wind velocities. If the latter were fairly accurate, we might not be too far off track. I explained my predicament to the pilot and dared to suggest that he might oblige me by flying for a short time at least, a little below the cloud that was masking all my precious headlands and other landmarks, but he adamantly refused. I didn't blame him. Safety must always come first in the air.

We first flew south, hopefully towards Fishguard in Wales. I had calculated an estimated time of arrival (ETA) and when it was that time, and the overall stratus cloud was still obstinately blocking our view below, I had to assume that we were there. I therefore gave the pilot another course calculated to take us to Belfast. Although this was also based on my flight plan, I clung to the hope that at some stage the cloud might clear and enable me to navigate in the way I had planned, and fix our precise position.

Winds blowing around the Irish Sea can be very fickle, suddenly changing, in speed or direction, or both. We knew that we might have been blown substantially off course. And that was the case.

Navigators were never to consider themselves lost, whatever the situation. Their circle of uncertainty simply widened, as emphasised in some of the notes for navigators. However, I was beginning to feel increasingly doubtful about our exact position.

Then, quite suddenly I wasn't. Just ahead of us, the sky began to clear, and almost immediately afterwards, both the pilot and we trainee navigators observed, to our consternation, puffs of smoke appearing in the sky in front of us. And wasn't that a city looming up some way ahead? Almost immediately, and concurrently, we all realised with horror the awful truth. We were wildly off course and had in fact entered the air space of a neutral country, the Republic of Ireland, which was expressing its displeasure in a most unfriendly way. We were at the receiving end of a shot across the bows! Ahead I could now discern the city of Dublin, a few miles away. Aircraft involved in the war with Germany – even a harmless little Anson – were clearly not welcome. Our pilot took the hint and immediately altered course 180 degrees.

But all was not lost. In fact, my spirits rose. Significantly off course though we were, I now had my fix – over Dublin. Using the air plot I had kept, I could now calculate the wind velocity and, on that basis, work out a new course for the pilot that would take us to Belfast.

Happily the visibility continued to improve and I was able to get another fix when crossing the coast of County Down. The wind had veered another 7 degrees but its speed had hardly changed. I gave a new course to the pilot, who was quite pleased that he now had an active navigator on board. So was I. Sometime later, my morale soared when we arrived over Belfast at almost exactly the ETA that I had calculated, and we were soon back at Jurby.

It wasn't the most auspicious start to my career as a navigator but at least I didn't have stratus cloud throughout the entire flight. I was also grateful to Dublin for confirming our position so positively, even though their reception, when we inadvertently invaded Irish air space, could have been more polite. However, I now had to steel myself for a debriefing with the dreaded Flight Lieutenant Biss.

I fully expected an earful and with a degree of trepidation I knocked on the door of his office. After a minute or two, a voice bade me enter. I did so, and stood before him, only to be ignored for several minutes while he pretended to scrutinise some papers on his desk. Finally, he looked up, and requested my logbook and chart.

He glared at them for several minutes and it was some time before he looked up. Then with his face red and angry he tore several strips off me and made it abundantly clear that he was not at all impressed that we had flown into neutral Irish air space. My first navigational exercise was assessed as a D. Before the flight I had hoped for a B plus.

Then there was a quite unexpected development. His face suddenly crinkled into a truly benevolent smile, his expression that of a kind uncle, and he offered me words of advice and encouragement. He ended by assuring me that he was confident that I would be able to get a significantly improved assessment next time. Unbelievable. I felt elated, in spite of the D.

To a surprising degree, the spirits of all trainee navigators depended on those assessments. We wanted to be fully qualified navigators at the end of our course, with the promotion and wing emblem (brevet) that went with it. Also, of course, we wanted to be highly skilled at the job.

Many months later, as a trained navigator and part of a crew, I first navigated Wellingtons, and then Lancasters, on many flights. But then, whether I was using radio, radar or the stars, cloud cover below the aircraft was never a problem. In fact it was irrelevant.

I often thought about Flight Lieutenant Biss. Perhaps he really wasn't a bad sort, just someone very anxious to maintain standards – in his own way.

★ ★ ★

Low cloud, and an absence of reliable aids, could make air navigation problematic even for experienced navigators, as illustrated in these two examples.

It may have been relatively rare for a navigator to be completely lost while on operations, especially over Europe, but in other parts of the world it was not at all unknown and for very good reasons.

Tom Winup, a bomb aimer and fellow ACA member, was on special duties in the Far East, doing work of a similar kind to George Smith (see Chapter 10). His aircraft had to take agents (British, Americans and Eurasians) and supplies eastwards, from India to French Indo-China (as it was) – an enormous distance. All the crew were experienced. These were secret operations. Some of the flights took twenty-four hours and meant that the aircraft had to be weighed down with extra fuel tanks, which to a degree replaced armament. Since the aircraft would have to fly over Japanese-occupied territory, with little means of defence, these were very risky operations indeed, quite apart from weather-related dangers of the kind described elsewhere. On one flight he described the weather as 'awful':

> We never saw the ground for eight hours because of cloud, but we had to get there. As we approached the area to do the drop of supplies to the French by parachute, all our powers of navigation, and the pilot's flying skills were needed.

There were obviously no radar navigation aids, and no help was available from the radio, so they had been forced to rely on map reading, which of course was impossible when they were above continuous cloud. After flying 'blind' for several hours, the weary pilot put a question to his navigator: 'Any idea where we are? Hazard a guess, navigator. Over land? Over sea?'

'No idea,' he admitted. The pilot descended until they were below cloud, and that was at 100ft.

'Over the sea,' said the navigator confidently.

'It's not what's below us I'm worried about,' replied the skipper. 'It's what's around us.'

On all sides were a number of volcanic islands, rising up well into the clouds, none of which were on their maps. Somehow, the aircraft had threaded its way between cloud-shrouded volcanoes. It was incredibly fortuitous that it hadn't crashed into one. That was one of many close encounters with death for the crew.

* * *

Finally, I learnt from the obituary of Air Commodore John Mitchell (*Daily Telegraph*, 12 February 2016) that he was the navigator of Churchill's personal aircraft during the Second World War (at first an Avro York) that was specially furnished with a boardroom, en suite lavatory, dining room and sleeping quarters. In that aircraft, Mitchell's navigational skills were employed in transporting Churchill to the many summit meetings of war leaders. He had to rely on long-range radio aids for the most part, but when on a long leg over the sea he depended largely on astronavigation. One must remember that most of Europe was occupied by Nazi Germany so the routes had to be carefully planned to circumvent hostile territory.

The flights could be very difficult. For instance, on 8 October 1944 Churchill visited Moscow. The aircraft had to fly via Cairo, though France was by then liberated. On the way, Mitchell had no radio aids to fix his position and the use of only inadequate maps. He was never actually lost but he must have had many moments of uncertainty as they encountered so much cloud.

Frequently meeting cloud, his aircraft had to fly very low so that he could see the ground, and sometimes the aircraft's height was far from ideal from a safety point of view. I'm sure that Mitchell must have been very concerned about that at times but Churchill would have been deeply immersed in discussions with his Chiefs of Staff and quite unaware of any potentially dangerous navigational problems.

However, it's interesting to me that at the time that, as a novice navigator, I was struggling to navigate an Avro Anson round the Irish Sea, the experienced navigator John Mitchell was navigating Churchill's Avro York to meet Joseph Stalin in Moscow. And although over land not sea, he was probably experiencing similar difficulties to those I met with: difficulty with map reading because of cloud cover and problems caused by the absence of other reliable navigation aids.

4

PUTTING AN AIRCREW TOGETHER

When qualified, all airmen were awarded their badges of competence – their brevets, or in the case of pilots, their wings – to be sewn on to their uniforms. It was a very proud moment after a long, and fairly intensive, period of training. We were also appropriately promoted in rank. All leading aircraftmen (LACs) during training, we were, in a single moment, promoted to either sergeant or pilot officer; and, all being well, after six months, the sergeants would be promoted to flight sergeants and the pilot officers to flying officers.

Now a qualified navigator, I returned to the mainland from the Isle of Man and awaited the crew-making process with pleasurable anticipation, coupled with a touch of apprehension. In particular, I wondered what sort of pilot I would be working with, because pilots and navigators needed to work very closely together for long periods in the air. Would he be someone with whom I could work happily and comfortably? A highly skilled pilot? A good captain with excellent leadership qualities? There would certainly be stressful and critical periods. Would he be good in an emergency?

All pilots became captains of their aircraft, irrespective of their rank in relation to that of the other crew members. Thus, a sergeant pilot would be captain of his aircraft even if, say, the navigator or rear gunner happened to be a pilot officer. To some that may seem strange but I have never heard of it causing any difficulty. It was fully accepted that the pilot must always be 'the skipper'.

A wartime crew needed to be a very well-integrated team, working together effectively and happily. Each member would be highly dependent on the others so unstinted support and cooperation were essential as well as good personal rapport.

Except for those pilots who were destined to fly in fighter aircraft, the newly qualified airmen would all be ready, and keen, to join a crew. A Mosquito needed a crew of two; a Wellington, five; a Lancaster, seven; and a Short Sunderland flying boat (which carried a cook) or a Flying Fortress, ten. Most new crews would first fly in a two-engine aircraft before moving to a four-engine heavy bomber at a Heavy Conversion Unit (HCU), such as Swinderby in Lincolnshire.

What, I wondered, would be the crew-bonding procedure? Would it be prescriptive or informal/voluntary? Letting my imagination have free rein, I could see a group of officers sitting round a table, examining records and pontificating:

Officer 1: 'This chap Lager seems to be a very reliable navigator but I see he's twice been drunk during his training period and was once in a brawl that resulted in some damage in the mess. What shall we do with him?'

Officer 2: 'Yes, he's actually a very good navigator but we'll have to place him very carefully. To be fair, he's never been the worse for wear in the air. Anyway, put him with a pilot who's mature and experienced.'

Officer 3: 'No problem there. Puttemdown fits the bill. If it's necessary, he'll quietly caution anyone in his crew whose behaviour is causing concern, and do it pleasantly and tactfully. He's a really effective leader. And since his hospitalisation has ended, he's free. His old crew now have another pilot.'

Officer 1: 'Great! Let's put them together.'

And so on.

The reality could not have been more different. The RAF appeared to be entirely unconcerned about who should fly with whom. Its policy for newly trained aircrews was to form them into crews without the slightest delay. The approved method was to let them sort it out for themselves – a DIY procedure.

Accordingly, we pilots, navigators, wireless operators, bomb aimers, etc. were all ushered into a large hall, where tea and biscuits were available. In a very short time, as new conversations broke out, with laughter exploding everywhere, the noise became almost deafening. Nearby, a pilot was shooting a line about his romantic episodes to a sceptical but amused audience. Further away, a hefty bomb aimer with a booming voice was describing how one of his faux bombs hit a cow. As often happens at large gatherings, there appeared to be more airmen talking than listening.

I was wondering whether I should infiltrate one of the many groups that had formed and, if so, which one, when I noticed two airmen making a bee line for me – a pilot and a bomb aimer – and when they arrived, the following conversation took place:

Pilot: 'I'm John, and this is Jack. We're both from Kent and we thought we'd form a Kentish crew. Are you from Kent?'

Me: 'I'm George and yes I am from Kent. My home's in Bromley, north-west Kent.'

Bomb aimer: 'Fine. So would you like to be our navigator?'

Me: 'Yes. Count me in.'

Jack and John were about my own age, and soon afterwards a wireless operator called Stan joined us. All three seemed to be friendly and keen to make new friends. While I was pleased to make their acquaintance, and glad that the process of 'crewing up' had begun, I felt that it was a very casual and unorganised way of forming a crew.

In fact it seemed a little bizarre. None of us had the least idea whether or not John was a first-class pilot with good leadership skills, and no one knew anything about my expertise (or lack of it) as a navigator, though arguably we were the two really key crew members, since our aircraft wouldn't be able to go anywhere without us working together harmoniously. Nor, of course, did we know anything about personal factors – our temperaments, our idiosyncrasies, and so on. We and other crew members would nevertheless be confined in a noisy, cramped, metal cylinder for hours on end, in which we would be subjected to various stresses and strains, and perhaps frequent dangers, when our interdependence could hardly be exaggerated.

We then discussed the question of an air gunner.

That was a turning point. Suddenly the criterion of location (Kent) that had apparently been of prime importance was now abandoned and replaced by that of competence, much to my amusement. In fact, there was never again any mention of a 'Kentish Crew'. The conversation went something like this:

John: 'We need to have the best rear gunner that we can get.'

Jack: 'That's right. Rear gunners are the main defence against night fighters. Tell you what. I'll find out who came top in his Gunnery School.'

John: 'Great idea! We'll get the best available gunner before someone else nabs him.'

This, I thought, is more like it. We were now talking about a vital aircrew task and the need for a highly skilled air gunner, who would be crucially important for our safety. At the same time, I smiled inwardly, because, in fact, we would all be highly interdependent and the skills of each of us would be essential for the safety of all of us.

I have no idea how Jack found the information he sought on air gunners and their level of expertise, but he soon returned with a diminutive Scot, who apparently satisfied the new selection criterion. Of course, we greeted him warmly and welcomed him into our team (crew).

But did any of us actually have anything in common? Perhaps only that we were all volunteers, who had opted to become members of an aircrew, we were all young and optimistic, and the world we had known for some years (it was 1944) was a world at war. We had come together to take part in it.

There would be five of us altogether to crew a Wellington. Later, we would crew a Lancaster, when we would need two new crew members: a flight engineer and a mid-upper gunner (and they didn't come from Kent either).

So how did this apparently odd DIY procedure actually work out? The answer is: surprisingly well. In our Wellington we each honed our specialist skills, and increasingly gelled into an effective team and a happy one. And we stayed that way.

★ ★ ★

My impression is that in the vast majority of cases, the above ad hoc way of 'crewing up' proved reasonably satisfactory.

Gerald Carver, several of whose death-defying experiences are recorded in Chapter 13, said of his crew:

> We got on well ... We were a mixed bunch – Scots, English, Canadian and Australian – and our survival was due to teamwork, vigilance, professional gunners, and a good slice of luck.

Of course, there were exceptions. Sometimes, crew members would learn that their pilot or some other member of the crew was not particularly skilful or reliable. Or there could be tensions caused by personality or psychological factors. At some stage there could be crew changes for any number of reasons. When a crew became operational, of course, crew changes might happen at any time through death or injury. A replacement would simply arrive to join an incomplete crew.

Don Foster, DFM, another fellow ACA member who completed forty-nine operations, was a wireless operator/gunner before becoming a pilot. In his earlier role, he has spoken about once having an excellent skipper and then having to fly with one who was entirely different:

> He never spoke a word to me after I had many times brought him home after a long, complicated and exhausting trip, with fixes and bearings – not a word. He scrambled

down after taxiing to the dispersal, jumped into the trans-port and drove off, leaving me to slog back to HQ on foot for debriefing.

And the last straw for Don was: 'All other skippers bought all their crew drinks – but not him.'

* * *

Especially overseas, crews were often formed of whoever was available, when airmen had no choice regarding their fellow crew members. For example, Tom Winup (mentioned earlier) was a bomb aimer based at one time in India on spe-cial (secret) duties. He has recalled his own experience of 'crewing up':

> We didn't have a choice ... I was put down with an Australian pilot, Flight Sergeant Porter, who struck me as a decent, dependable sort ... But then it was all changed, and I was put down to fly with an Irish pilot, Paddy Drummond, who had a reputation for being drunk most of the time when not flying ... As it turned out, Porter's crew crashed doing circuits and bumps. Had the change not been made I wouldn't be here to tell the tale.

* * *

For the very special task of taking part in Pathfinder opera-tions, crews were often headhunted. The Pathfinder squadrons of Bomber Command were responsible for target marking. If they did their job well, marking the target area with flares, it was much easier for the main bomber force to bomb accurately. The Pathfinder crews were normally equipped with the radar aid Oboe before other crews.

★ ★ ★

Finally, Geoff King DFC, bomb aimer/radar navigator, and another of our ACA members, completed fifty operations, several of them with a Pathfinder squadron. He was asked how he and his crew had managed to survive. He put it down primarily to the quality of the crew. To survive so many operations, involving inevitably several near disasters and many stressful situations, the crew must have been outstanding, though no doubt luck also played its part. It always did.

5

THE NIGHT I PUT MY FOOT IN IT

The Vickers Wellington was a twin-engine, long-range medium bomber designed in the mid 1930s at Brooklands (Britain's first international car racing track) by Vickers' Chief Designer Rex Pierson.

Its unique geodetic construction (described opposite) was by the brilliant Barnes Wallis (designer of the bouncing bombs used by the Dam Busters). It was the best bomber with which Britain entered the war.

Pilots managed time and time again to bring back from operations Wellingtons that had been battered by bullets, shells and cannon fire and were peppered with holes, including large areas of framework. The Wellington was often a survivor, and that meant its crews often survived, too.

In spite of its vulnerability to attack in the early years of the Second World War, when the weakness of its armaments were exposed by Luftwaffe fighter planes, the Wellington served Bomber Command well. With modifications, including machine guns firing from its beam, it was still in use, though no longer a front-line bomber, at the end of the war.

Following the piece below, which explains, inter alia, how the aircraft was put together, are two rather special Wellington stories.

* * *

My own Wellington story is not very special, being more a confession, but those that follow are about outstanding initiatives and inspiring bravery displayed by Wellington crews.

Though I fully appreciated the virtues of the Wellington, as a navigator I was never entirely comfortable in it. I found it too dark and cramped. I well remember how thrilled I was when we first flew in a Lancaster, and I noted how much more light there was and how spacious the table was on which I could set out my Mercator chart and all my accessories: square protractor, Dalton computer, sextant, pencils, ruler, compasses, eraser, and so on.

Then there was the incident in that aircraft that I am about to describe that was entirely my fault, but which hardly enhanced my affection for it.

To appreciate the incident fully, you need to understand two things: firstly, how a Wellington, known affectionately by its crew as the Wimpey, and by the disrespectful as the Flying Coffin, was constructed, and secondly, what I was doing walking along its fuselage in the blackness of the night – and quite alone.

Firstly, I'll briefly outline the mode of construction of the Wellington.

Imagine two spirals, made of duralumin – a kind of aluminium – one inside the other. Where they touch they are riveted together. That, in essence, in the simplest of terms, describes the incredibly resilient airframe – the Wellington's geodetic (or basket weave) construction: a diagonal, crisscross metal framework, like a trellis. That skeleton was covered by Irish linen, which was then given several coats of dope, a type of varnish, until it was quite stiff and firm.

The result was an aircraft that held together very well when blasted with anti-aircraft fire or attacked with cannon by night fighters. It might be holed in several places, yet remain stubbornly airborne. No wonder crews returning safely from operations with a 'moth-eaten' aircraft were forever grateful for the Wellington's amazing strength and resilience.

But, in spite of its many virtues, the Wellington was obsolete to a degree even in the early days of the war when enemy defences were being probed. In December 1939, twenty-four of them attacked Schillig Roads in Lower Saxony, Germany. Nine were shot down, three ditched in the sea and three were too badly damaged to return.

Such losses of its best bomber, early in the war, must have shaken the chiefs of Bomber Command.

The Wellington's fabric was not designed to bear the weight of a human being directly; nor was the duralumin frame. Therefore a reinforced area, consisting of a wooden plank, ran along the floor of the aircraft. If anyone walked the Wellington's length, he had to be very careful to tread only on that reinforced area.

I never walked along the length of the fuselage while we were flying (just as well you may think, when you've read a little further). I was always fully immersed in navigating the aircraft.

However, on the ground, and in the middle of the night, I had no choice. Well before take-off, I had to walk along to the rear of the Wellington to check the compass, to ensure that it was functioning correctly. It was the master compass and was located as far away as possible from all magnetic influences that could distort its reading. Most such influences are obviously around the front of the aircraft. The pilot used a slave compass.

A superb photograph taken head-on of a loose group of Wellingtons. Wellingtons had two radial engines and were armed with two machine guns at the front and two at the rear. Later, two more machine guns were mounted at the beam (waist) position. Yet there were always large defenceless angles. (SDASM archives)

Some time before a training flight, in the middle of winter, at about 2 a.m., and holding a small pinpoint torch, I made my way towards the rear of the aircraft. As I walked gingerly on the reinforced strip, in pitch-black darkness, I sensed the familiar smell of wartime aircraft – a mixture of dope, paint and oil – seemingly more penetrating in the blackness of the night.

I had completed this task many times before, and always tried to be very careful to plant my feet squarely on the reinforced plank.

But on this occasion, when I was very close to the compass, and near to the end of the fuselage, it happened. My right foot slipped, I lost my balance and, to my dismay, my foot suddenly crashed through the fabric comprising the floor of the aircraft.

I cannot recall how deeply my lower limb fell. It all happened in 1944. There is, in fact, plenty of room between the duralumin struts for the whole leg to be swallowed up, but I think I was able to withdraw my foot without too much difficulty. And I'm rather glad that it all happened on the ground and not in the air!

I was guilty of making the Wellington unserviceable, and I would have to face the music. Our crew would not have the training flight that had been planned, and it was sackcloth and ashes for me.

★ ★ ★

That incident may be said to highlight a negative aspect of the Wellington's construction. However, the co-pilot of a Wellington, Sergeant James Ward, a shy New Zealander based at RAF Feltwell in Norfolk, made good use of the latticed metal construction of the wings when an extreme emergency arose.

On 7 July 1941, following a bombing raid on Munster, a German night fighter, a Messerschmitt 110, attacked the Wellington, causing the fuel tank in the starboard wing to be opened. A fire began at the rear of the engine. That was obviously extremely dangerous. The fuel tank could explode at any time. Following unsuccessful efforts by all the crew to put out the fire, Sergeant Ward decided that the only way was to go directly up to it and then to try to put it out manually. If he failed to do that, and fairly quickly, the crew would have to bail out.

He managed to climb through the narrow astrodome (used for sextant 'shots') on the end of a rope in case he should slip.

Buffeted by the wind, he then kicked or tore holes in the aircraft's wing fabric with a fire axe to give himself hand and foot holds. He reached the engine fire and finally succeeded in smothering the flames and putting them out completely, though the fuel continued to leak. However, the Wellington, although holed, was now safe and so were the crew.

It was more dangerous for Ward, now extremely tired, and still at the mercy of a powerful slipstream, to return to the fuselage, than it had been when leaving it, but with the navigator's help he got back safely inside the fuselage.

The aircraft made a successful emergency landing at Newmarket in Suffolk. As a result of the amazing courage of Sergeant Ward, both the crew and the aircraft were saved.

Sergeant James Ward was awarded the Victoria Cross for his gallant action. The full story is in the *London Gazette* of 5 August 1941:

On the night of 7th July 1941, Sergeant Ward was second pilot of a Wellington returning from an attack on Munster. When flying over the Zuider Zee at 13,000 feet, the aircraft was attacked from beneath by a Messerschmitt, which secured hits with cannon shell and incendiary bullets. The rear gunner was wounded in the foot but delivered a burst of fire, which sent the enemy fighter down, apparently out of control. Fire then broke out near the starboard engine and, fed by petrol from a split pipe, quickly gained an alarming hold and threatened to spread to the entire wing. The crew made strenuous efforts to reduce the fire with extinguishers … but without success. They were then warned to be ready to abandon the aircraft.

As a last resort, Sergeant Ward volunteered to make an attempt to smother the fire with an engine cover. At first he proposed to discard his parachute to reduce wind resistance, but was finally persuaded to take it. A rope was tied to him, though this was of little help and might have become a danger had he been blown off the aircraft. With the help of the navigator, he then climbed through the narrow astro-hatch and put on his parachute.

Breaking the [aircraft's] fabric to make hand and foot holds where necessary, Sergeant Ward succeeded in descending three feet to the wing and proceeding another 3ft to a position behind the engine, despite the slipstream from the airscrew, which nearly blew him off the wing. Lying in this precarious position, he smothered the fire in the wing fabric … Tired as he was, he was able with the navigator's assistance, to make successfully the perilous journey back into the aircraft.

The flight home had been made possible by the gallant action of Sergeant Ward in extinguishing the fire on the wing, in circumstances of the greatest difficulty and at the risk of his life.

Sadly, James Ward died only ten weeks after his VC action, when his Wellington bomber was hit by flak over its target and caught fire. Only two of the crew survived.

★ ★ ★

The second Wellington story comes from a fellow ACA member, Gerald Carver. Gerald (some of whose other experiences are recorded in Chapter 13) described an incident in October 1941, when he was piloting a Wellington.

Several Wellingtons were to take off for Crete. Gerald's aircraft was to be first off, heavily laden, like the others, with high explosives and incendiary bombs.

In view of the aircraft's now considerable weight, Gerald kept it low as it left the runway in order to build up speed before climbing away, as was normal practice.

When he was no more than 15ft above ground there was an ear-splitting explosion and flames were seen on the left.

The port undercarriage had struck something. Gerald's aircraft came back to earth rapidly and violently, shaking up all the crew.

A petrol bowser had been carelessly left on some grass at the end of the runway. Struck by the undercarriage of the rapidly accelerating but low-flying aircraft, it had exploded, and bombs had been scattered everywhere.

It was a miracle the aircraft had not gone up with the petrol bowser, as crews just behind feared. The aircraft finally came to a standstill and to everyone's amazement the crew were unharmed, except that Gerald had a cut under his left eye that needed three stitches.

For all the crew, this was a very close encounter with death and not the first.

6

THERE'S A LAYER OF ICE ON MY CHART

AND SOME ACCOUNTS OF OTHER AIRMEN'S EXPERIENCES OF EXTREME ICY CONDITIONS

Britain's most successful wartime heavy bomber was the four-engine Lancaster, which had seven crew members. When damaged severely in action, it often remained airborne. It could fly quite well on three engines, stay safely airborne on two, and had even been known to land on one.

Its most famous raid was the Dam Busters attack but there were many others equally dangerous such as the raid on Germany's secret research installation at Peenemünde in north Germany, where the flying bombs known as 'doodlebugs' (V1s) and the rocket-propelled bombs (V2s) were designed and developed, under the direction of Dr Wernher von Braun.

The Lancaster's speed when flying level with a full load was 275mph, and when at an altitude in excess of 20,000ft its speed was about 200mph. With a full bomb load, its range was over 1,500 miles.

This shows very clearly the main characteristics of the Lancaster, including the four Rolls-Royce Merlin engines, the gun turrets, the twin fins and rudders, the pilot's cabin and the astrodome, etc. (SDASM archives, Charles Daniels collection)

Some 7,377 Lancasters were built and it entered service in 1942. Around 3,500 of them were lost on operations and another 200 of them crashed or were written off. Of the remainder, the vast majority were scrapped.

As a result, Britain can today put only one Lancaster into the air, and there is another one in Canada.

I had a rather extraordinary experience as a navigator in a Lancaster in 1944–45. It was a long flight and I was using the stars to fix our position. I suppose the event was a trifle hazardous, but no one suffered at all, and, when related afterwards, its unorthodox aspects attracted much merriment among fellow airmen.

The European war had ended, and my very efficient radar aids, H2S and Gee, were removed soon afterwards. Radar had a limited range – about 400 miles – and it was considered that for the war in the Pacific, it would be fairly useless (although an American radar system called Loran was being used there). Our crew had been earmarked for that war. We would need to fly very long distances, and I would depend entirely on the stars.

Therefore I had to brush up my skills with the sextant, and astronavigation procedures.

I welcomed the switch to the stars. It involved more work than using radar aids, it took longer to fix our position, it required very careful calculations, and it was less accurate. On the other hand, the night sky at 20,000–25,000ft is superb: a firmament of stars sparkling like a myriad diamonds. The task of selecting three of them to fix our position, and then 'shooting them' with a sextant, was both absorbing and aesthetically pleasurable. And there is nothing to obscure these most dependable of navigation aids, at heights of over 20,000ft, the occasional appearance of wispy, silk-like strands of ice crystals (cirrus) simply adding to the beauty of the heavens.

At some stage in my early navigation training, I had absorbed the fact that air temperature drops 3 degrees Fahrenheit for every thousand feet of added height or altitude. That can only be approximate, and we're all using Celsius these days, but it's a nice round figure – and easy to remember.

As Mount Everest is about 29,000ft, the surrounding air should register a temperature of something like 87 degrees Fahrenheit below sea level temperature, and around our Lancaster aircraft, flying at a height of around 22,000ft, it would have been about 66 degrees below that.

Though the Lancaster was always cold in some parts, most of us kept reasonably warm. We usually wore kapok suits under our flying gear, and our flying boots were cosy enough. However, the heating system had a limited effectiveness, and did not extend equally to every part of the aircraft. The worst off was the rear gunner in his isolated little turret, jutting out between the twin rudders in the rear, where he kept a lonely vigil. There were occasions when the temperature there could be minus 40 degrees Celsius, and cases of frostbite were not uncommon. Rear gunners usually wore heated suits, which often seem to have been ineffective. Imagine sitting in freezing conditions, feeling isolated from other crew members, in pitch-black darkness and in a cramped turret with little space to move.

The pilot, the flight engineer and I were normally comfortable enough but the wireless operator, sitting just under the source of heat, could be too warm. There were occasions when he could actually be in a sweat. He sometimes flew in his battledress.

Then, quite suddenly, we were all in the same boat – equally cold, freezing cold.

We were flying at around 23,000ft when I became aware that the temperature had dropped significantly. That can happen very quickly in an all-metal aircraft devoid of any insulating material. Yet I didn't notice the severe cold at first, being deeply immersed in the many tasks of my trade. Then I was forced to. I saw that a film of ice was covering my chart, giving it a shiny surface – and a very hard one. Moreover, the ice was thickening, as my breathing added to the humidity level. A large cluster of icicles had formed under my oxygen mask, and they were growing longer every minute. I remember instinctively breaking off some of them but they soon grew again. Water dripped down from them on to my chart, spread momentarily, then immediately froze again. Our heating system seemed to have failed utterly, leaving us to endure polar conditions.

It happened at a particularly awkward time for me (although I can't think when it might not have been awkward), as I wanted to plot some lines on my Mercator chart, the vectors for a new triangle of velocities, so that I could calculate an up-to-date wind velocity and a new course, air speed and ETA for the pilot.

How could I draw anything on my chart when it was covered with ice? It didn't help that I was beginning to feel very cold. I never wore gloves or mittens when flying, preferring to handle everything, including chart work, and star shooting with the sextant, without any encumbrances, and now my fingers were beginning to lose feeling and manipulative ability.

Looking back, I'm surprised I didn't make more use of the hand-held Dalton computer that we usually carried aboard. It was a kind of circular slide rule, which was a useful dead-reckoning instrument since it could be used to calculate courses, ground speed and ETA. I certainly used it before a flight to obtain that information, based, of course, on the forecast wind speed and direction.

Instinctively pressing on regardless of the ice, I selected one of the 2H pencils that I hadn't used so far on the flight. It was a spare one, and the hard, sharply chiselled point would perhaps cut through the ice so that my work could continue uninterrupted. Wishful thinking. Even though I pressed hard on the pencil, whilst hoping the point wouldn't break off, I managed only to raise a dense little cloud of tiny ice particles, which appeared to float in a cloud before settling on to my chart, and the pencil hadn't even reached its surface.

At that point, our Skipper's voice broke through the intercom:

'Skipper here. I'm afraid the heating system has broken down completely and Flight Engineer can't repair it. Are you all OK?'

'You are? I don't believe it. You must all be freezing. I know I am. Navigator, how is it affecting you? Is the present course OK?'

'Navigator here, Skip. I've just fixed our position and want to work out a new course but there's a problem. My chart is covered by a layer of ice. It's pretty hard. I thought my 2H pencil would cut through it. It didn't. I'm going to try a 4H now.'

'Skip here. OK George. Get back to me as soon as you can.'

'Skip, bomb aimer here. I've just had a word with Scotty [rear gunner]. He's very cold, blue in the face and shivering. I've given him some hot coffee and a blanket. He says he's OK.'

'Skipper here. Good, Jack. Everyone move as much as you can to keep your circulation going. I'm going to take us down a little but it'll still be pretty cold.'

I took out one of my 4H pencils, which I hardly ever use, and pressed it into action. Would it cut through the ice, or would the point break off? If that didn't work I had no alternative plan in mind.

The result exceeded my expectations. My knife-like pencil cut easily through the ice, producing a much more spectacular cloud of tiny ice particles than before, and I was able to draw a line on the chart. Admittedly it now looked a mess, as the ice hadn't travelled very far. There was a substantial pile of tiny, powdery chips covering most of it, which I just blew away. The chart remained covered by hard ice, but I was now able to cut right through it, and draw the lines that I needed to continue my work. After a few minutes, I contacted the pilot:

'Skip. Navigator here. Good news. I've managed to carry on using my chart and I have a new course. Change to 265 degrees and 245 knots.'

'Skip here. Good, George, and will that take us home?'

'Navigator. No, Skip. We've got another 150 miles to go and I'm sure we'll need to change course again before long as the wind is still veering.'

In spite of our lower altitude, the interior of our aircraft retained its polar appearance for the remainder of the flight, the heating system remaining out of order, and we all felt the cold. Nevertheless, everyone carried on as usual, though we must have looked a wretchedly uncomfortable bunch.

The stars sparkled magnificently above us and I continued to 'shoot' them in the usual way. With their help, I regularly fixed our position and calculated new courses. Though the cold conditions were a little dispiriting, my overwhelming feeling was of relief and satisfaction that I was able to work almost normally in spite of what had happened. In fact, I felt rather pleased, as one does when a problem has been overcome. Provided I blew the powered ice away every time I drew a line, and sometimes several times whilst drawing a single line, my chart remained tidy, and workable, and I was able to supply our skipper with our latest position, new courses, air speeds and ETAs. And now and then I broke a few more icicles off my oxygen mask to reduce its dribbling.

Perhaps surprisingly, in spite of the cold, I didn't have a hot drink or eat anything. Neither food nor drink ever entered my head, and I never took a thermos flask with me. Even on long flights of ten hours or so, I didn't feel a need to drink or eat anything while I was navigating. I was far too busy. In any case, one doesn't usually eat in the middle of the night. Of course, we were well fed both before every flight, usually with eggs, bacon, tomatoes and fried potatoes, and a similar meal would be available on our return.

In the official publication *Bomber Command* (page 80) there is mention of crew rations in a paper bag containing 'a few biscuits, an apple or orange, a bar of chocolate, some barley sugar, chewing gum and raisins'. Not very exciting. I think I would probably have brought them back untouched, though in an emergency, such as a forced landing or ditching in the sea, they would have proved useful.

Throughout a flight, I remained seated in front of the chart on my table, ensconced in my curtained 'office', except for moving to the astrodome – not far away – to 'shoot' the stars I had selected, and I was hardly aware of two potentially useful facilities in our Lancaster: a rest bed and an Elsan closet (which, happily, I never had to use).

I had expected quite soon to navigate our Lancaster to the island of Okinawa in the Pacific Ocean, from where, as part of Operation TIGER FORCE, we would attack Japanese mainland targets (see Chapter 18). In the event, of course, the dropping of atom bombs on Hiroshima and Nagasaki made our eastward flight unnecessary. In the meantime, however, our crew went on long training flights with the Pacific very much in mind.

My priority was always to keep feeding the pilot with the information he needed, especially our position, changes of course and airspeed. On this occasion, that information depended on the capacity of a 4H pencil to cut through a layer of ice settling firmly on my chart.

When I explained what had happened to the other crew members, all of us, 19-year-old flight sergeants at the time, laughed uproariously, as we exchanged accounts. The icing up of our aircraft had been problematic for each of us and we'd all had to work out our different solutions. Ours was the laughter of shared relief. In spite of a spell of polar conditions in the aircraft, we had pressed on and it had all worked out pretty well.

★ ★ ★

One crew member who normally carried with him a thermos of coffee was the rear gunner. Usually the coldest one in the aircraft, he often used coffee not only for drinking, but also to thaw out his guns when it was particularly cold.

A former rear gunner, one of our ACA members, Ron Liversage MBE (38, 101, 148 and 625 Squadrons), wouldn't fly without a thermos of coffee. Here is his own account (not completely in his own words) of what happened one night at a time when he was quite inexperienced:

Flying in a Lancaster, and on the way to a target in Germany, the temperature was minus 38 degrees Celsius, so I was very cold and, of course, in pitch-black darkness. Then, just as the navigator announced that we were 20 minutes from the target, there was an explosion in my turret, and I instinctively fired a protective arc round the rear of the aircraft.

Then I felt something warm and wet running down my leg. I reported to the captain that I had been hit and was bleeding, and asked for permission to turn on the tiny turret light to assess the extent of my injuries. I then made a discovery that was a bit embarrassing. The intense cold had caused my coffee flask to explode. The lid had been blown off and the warm coffee was running down my leg. I wasn't wounded and there was no enemy in sight, but I would need to get a new thermos flask!

Ron completed a tour of thirty operations in Lancasters, and towards the end of the European war was involved in Operation MANNA (see Chapter 17).

★ ★ ★

Many aspects of the weather could be of crucial importance to flying operations in the Second World War but icing was often a particularly serious problem.

In the early years of the war, when the main aircraft of Bomber Command were Whitleys, Blenheims, Hampdens, Battles and Wellingtons, the weather was often a major factor in the success of an operation. Only a small number of bombers were ever available and they frequently had to operate at their maximum range in atrocious weather.

Freezing conditions occurred on a leaflet raid by a Whitley aircraft, in the Dusseldorf area, in October 1939. The temperature was between minus 22 and minus 33 degrees Celsius. Ice on the wings was 6in thick, a considerable threat to the aircraft's lift. Then the starboard engine caught fire and had to be switched off. The aircraft went into a dive. Both pilots tried together to pull up its nose to arrest the dive but were unsuccessful until the aircraft was down to 7,000ft. Then they discovered that both the rudder and elevators were immovable, presumably still iced up, while the aircraft was descending at 2,000ft a minute. The port engine then stopped and in spite of the rapid descent there was still 4in of ice protruding from the engine cowling and much ice elsewhere including the windscreens, which were thickly coated.

At one point the order to bail out was given, but as no reply was received from either of the gunners, the order was cancelled. Afterward it emerged that both were unconscious: the front gunner from a blow on the head from an ammunition magazine and the rear gunner from a blow on the head from the turret, during the dive.

The aircraft emerged from cloud into heavy rain at an altitude of 200ft and brushed through the tops of trees. Finally, the second pilot managed to crash-land it in a field in France. The crew, all safe, spent the night in the damaged aircraft and in the morning were looked after by some French people.[1]

* * *

Icing problems could be particularly bad when our aircraft carried out raids in parts of Norway, which was, of course, occupied by Germany. Below is an account of a Blenheim on the way to an attack on military targets in Stavanger:

> At 13,000ft, the engines of two of the Blenheims became iced up and stopped. One of them dropped more or less out of control until only about 600ft above the sea, when they started again. The other Blenheim … actually struck the waves at the very moment its engines came to life … both aircraft got safely back.[2]

* * *

Icing could cause a serious communication problem, and that's what happened on the very first day of the war, 3 September 1939. A single Blenheim with its crew of three set out from the RAF station at Wyton to photograph units of the German fleet around Wilhelmshaven. Photography and reconnaissance were completed successfully, but it was not possible to communicate the information to the Admiralty because, flying at 24,000ft, the wireless set froze. It was only when the Blenheim had arrived at back at Wyton that the Admiralty was made aware of the war's first target, whether for the RAF or the navy.[3]

* * *

A Wellington pilot, Geoff Cole DFC, of our ACA branch recalled flying home in 1940 following a raid on Dusseldorf. He decided to climb over some very extensive cloud and at 14,000ft had a shock. Both engines had suddenly stopped working. They were iced up. The aircraft was fitted with a hand-operated alcohol pump that was supposed to de-ice both engines and this was operated urgently and with some desperation. Unfortunately it didn't work and the aircraft began to glide, constantly losing height. Without power the pilot had no control over the Wellington, and as the downward slide continued saw no alternative at 6,000ft than to order the crew to put on their parachutes and prepare to jump. Then, to everyone's surprise, the starboard engine started. The aircraft was now below 4,000ft and Geoff said, 'We're OK. We can keep going on one engine.'

He was rather optimistic. The aircraft continued to lose height and was soon at 2,000ft, and over the North Sea. At one stage they were flying at 500ft. Then suddenly the port engine burst into life, and Geoff spoke to his crew again: 'We've now got both engines going. I'll increase height and you can all relax.'

* * *

Finally, to complete this icy chapter, here is a brief account of the experience of another of our ACA members, Ken Dixon (816, 854 and 857 Squadrons) who was an observer (early name for navigators) in the Fleet Air Arm. He was flying in one of the anti-submarine Swordfish aircraft on a carrier, escorting a Russian convoy bound for Murmansk. A cruiser and seventeen destroyers were also in the escort. All were

A Lancaster B. III in flight. (RAF/Wikimedia Commons)

needed because fourteen U-boats, with torpedoes ready, were waiting for them as well as Junkers 88 dive-bombers.

A danger almost as threatening came from the bitterly cold, icy conditions. The Swordfish had to land on an icy deck, which pitched and rolled in very rough seas and blizzard conditions. Some of the landing equipment seized up, as did the guns. There was also the constant danger of ice building up on the wings during flight, and of course, there was ice covering every exposed part of every ship.

On this occasion one destroyer, the *Mahratta*, was torpedoed and sank with only seventeen of the 200 crew surviving. One cargo ship was torpedoed on the return journey. Two U-boats (U-4722 and U-355) were hit by rockets and sank.

However, this operation (and other similar ones) was successfully completed. The Russians received much-needed war materials and later presented all the sailors and airmen in Allied ships and aircraft with medals.

The convoys, to supply Russia with food, equipment and materials essential for her war effort against Germany, have probably not had the attention they merit.

NOTES

1 *Bomber Command*, page 33
2 *Bomber Command*, page 38
3 *Bomber Command*, page 7

7

THE NIGHT OUR CREW WERE STARVED OF OXYGEN

This oxygen 'tis useful stuff,
Provided that you have enough,
But if you have too little,
You'll topple like a skittle.

Anon

There are two facts that everyone knows about oxygen: that the amount of the gas in the air diminishes progressively with height and that oxygen is vital to life. More than a few minutes without it can cause damage to the brain, heart and other organs, leading to unconsciousness and death.

We wartime airmen were always told that at 10,000ft our efficiency would diminish unless we wore an oxygen mask. At 15,000ft the lack of oxygen could be dangerous. We usually wore our masks not long after take-off while our aircraft climbed to 20,000ft or more. Otherwise, with plenty to think about, we might have forgotten to put them on.

Yet people sometimes climb high mountains without an oxygen supply – even Everest at over 29,000ft. It would seem that the body could make some adjustment if the ascent is gradual. When climbing Everest, consolidation at the various camps en route enables a partial adaptation to take place.

But no more than that. I remember seeing a newsreel of Everest climbers without oxygen masks, and they were gasping desperately, drawing in huge draughts of air in order to capture a little oxygen, while simultaneously expending huge amounts of energy. Their oxygen intake couldn't possible have matched their need for it. Brain damage can occur when the supply of oxygen does not meet the demand for it, which of course increases significantly during a strenuous climb. Lack of oxygen not only slows down the mind, but also causes muscle fatigue and loss of concentration.

It is true that there are parts of the world where people spend all their lives at heights of 12,000ft or more, including Tibet. One must assume that their organs have evolved so that they are comfortably adapted to cope with their environment.

We were flying back to base at night when it happened but I didn't notice for a time that anything was wrong. Oxygen deprivation is a silent, insidious killer that easily overcomes its unwary victims because, initially, the effect is like mild intoxication. One becomes pleasantly drowsy and only half aware of symptoms such as a tingling of the skin, a headache, a growing drowsiness – and perhaps a feeling of euphoria.

It did occur to me that I was becoming rather lethargic, but, though my concentration was fading, I carried on working, probably taking twice as long as usual to perform every task. I was completely oblivious of any danger and quite relaxed.

In a short time, if one is flying without oxygen at over 20,000ft, vision deteriorates, the engine sounds are hardly heard, breathing becomes laboured, the heart beats rapidly, lips and the skin under fingernails turn blue (and later the complexion), words are slurred, and there is a shortage of breath.

A reduced supply of oxygen to brain tissue is called cerebral hypoxia. When the supply is cut off completely, as in our case, further symptoms of this condition soon develop such as decreased motor control and inability to think clearly with both being particularly dangerous, of course, especially for the pilot and navigator.

Later still, if appropriate action is not taken, cerebral hypoxia results in unconsciousness, and then brain death. At 22,000ft, one can normally remain conscious for only five to ten minutes.

Some of our crew may well have been close to losing consciousness when the skipper's voice broke through the intercom and brought us all back to reality: 'Skipper here. Wakey! Wakey! Is everyone OK? The oxygen supply is kaput. No one's getting any. Flight Engineer says he can't get it going. I'm going to take us down to 6,000ft.'

Skip didn't waste any time. He lowered the nose of our Lancaster and put it into a rapid descent, while we were all pretty subdued. Though deprived of oxygen, we remained quite relaxed because it had made us light-headed, confused and disorientated. However, Skip was, thankfully, still capable of thinking clearly, and of taking appropriate action.

Once the new altitude was achieved, all seven of us began gradually to recover. We took off our now-useless oxygen masks and chatted noisily, laughing with relief that all was well – as we began to appreciate that we had just had a fortunate escape.

Unusually, some of us then left our positions and assembled around the skipper's cabin. There was the bomb aimer

(Jack), the navigator (me), the flight engineer (Tom), the wireless operator (Stan) and the pilot (John). We wanted to have a brief conflab and be assured that each one of us was in reasonably good shape. At first we just looked at one another and leg-pulled. Then Skip ran his eye over each of us in turn in a brief appraisal:

Skip: 'My God, that was a really dicey experience. Is everyone OK?'

Stan : [laughing] 'Well, we don't *look* OK. Look at us! We all look pretty horrible. We've got blue lips and blue fingernails, and we're as pale as ghosts. Some of us have bluish faces. I wouldn't like my girlfriend to see me now.'

Tom: 'Don't worry. We won't tell her.'

Stan: 'I'm not feeling too bad. At this altitude we should soon recover, shouldn't we?'

Skip: 'I'm sure we will, but is anyone feeling sick?'

We all assured Skip that we were recovering well.

Skip: 'Good. [speaking now in the intercom] Bill [mid-upper gunner], what about you?'

Bill: 'I'm OK, Skip. I'm just not thinking clearly, I'm feeling sleepy, and I've got blue fingernails like everyone else, but I'll be as right as rain in a few minutes.'

Skip: 'Fine, Bill. Now [with a change of tone] Navigator is this course going to take us back to base?'

Me: 'No, Skip, it would probably take us west of the Outer Hebrides, to nowhere in particular, except the Atlantic [laughter all round]. The wind has changed.'

Skip: 'Right. Then are you well enough to work out a new course to get us back to base?'

Me: 'Yes, Skip. The stars are still there. I'll fix our position, find out the latest wind velocity and work out a new course as quickly as I can.'

Skip: 'Good. Jack, would you take a look to see if Scotty [rear gunner] is OK?'

Jack: [just returned] 'Skip, Scotty's gone quite blue, his teeth are chattering and he's been sick. He's reacted to the lack of oxygen more than the rest of us, and I think he's feeling very cold, but he says he's OK.'

Skip: 'OK. Would you get back to him, Jack, and help him clean up. Then I'll have a word with him. The main thing is we're all OK, more or less, so let's get back to work.'

Scotty: 'Rear gunner here, Skip. I'll be glad of Jack's help, but I really am OK. I may look a bit dodgy but I'm getting better.'

Skip: 'That's great, Scotty. I'll buy you a drink when we get back.'

Me: 'I think a drink would be welcomed by all of us.'

Skip: 'Quite right, George. I'll buy you all a drink.'

We all recovered well and, in fact, carried on as if nothing had happened for the remainder of the flight, though we were much more subdued than usual, until we flew over our base, when our relief was manifest, and we all cheered without restraint. It was good to be home or almost home.

* * *

Much later I learnt further interesting facts about oxygen deprivation. Apparently, when the oxygen supply diminishes, the body responds initially by redirecting blood to the brain, but this increased flow cannot be more than doubled. After that, the reduced supply of oxygen to the brain tissue (cerebral hypoxia) begins to cause the symptoms, noted above, that all our crew experienced. Had our skipper not taken our Lancaster down to a lower altitude when he did, we would all have lost the ability to think clearly and we would have soon lost consciousness. Our brains demand priority in receiving oxygen.

Our crew was very fortunate to have a very competent pilot who was also a good leader, and his quick action on this occasion was much appreciated by all the crew.

* * *

It was not unknown for a crew to experience a failure of the oxygen supply combined with freezing conditions. On 1 October 1939 there was a leaflet raid on Berlin to inform its inhabitants of all the money stashed abroad by Nazi leaders. The weather was atrocious. In one Whitley aircraft, the oxygen system temporarily failed when it was flying at 22,500ft. Two of the crew collapsed. At the same time, part of the mechanism of the rear turret froze so that the gunner could not open his door. The navigator meanwhile dragged one of the collapsed crew to an oxygen supply, and tipped out most of the pamphlets, but shortly afterwards collapsed himself. The captain took the aircraft down to 9,000ft and at that height it was possible to open the rear turret door so the rear gunner was able to go to the assistance of the navigator, who was by then happily on the road to recovery.[1]

★ ★ ★

In another Whitley engaged in pamphlet dropping on the night of 27–28 October 1939 the oxygen supply broke down and the navigator and wireless operator were so affected that they had to lie down every few minutes. The heating system also failed and so oxygen deprivation was combined with frostbite, causing much distress. Even though the aircraft descended to 8,000ft the temperature did not improve and the icing condition grew worse, continuous movement of the controls becoming necessary to prevent them icing up. Nevertheless, the aircraft got back safely.[2]

NOTES

1 *Bomber Command*, page 31
2 *Bomber Command*, page 22

8

THE NIGHT I FLOATED LIKE AN ASTRONAUT

Me: 'Skip, Navigator here. I'm glad to be back at my desk.'

Skip: 'Why? Have you been shooting stars with your sextant?'

Me: 'No, Skip, I've been stuck to the roof of the aircraft and unable to do anything at all.'

Skip: 'You're kidding.'

Me: 'No. I'm not. When the kite dropped fairly rapidly a little while ago, I floated upwards until I reached the roof.'

Skip: 'My God. I didn't notice you up there. [laughing] I wish I'd seen you. Floating eh? Some people have all the luck. Are you OK?'

Me: 'Absolutely OK. I just floated upward, and after a while I floated down and back to my desk. It was quite remarkable.'

Skip: 'Amazing. Welcome back. I remember we dropped and lost quite a lot of height in an air pocket. I think I must have instinctively held on tightly to the controls. I must check that everyone else is OK. Have you still got all your bits and pieces?'

Me: 'Yes, Skip. Everything on my desk went up with me, and then returned with me. Nothing's missing.'

Skip: 'Incredible.'

I remember this incident vividly because it happened so suddenly, it was completely unexpected, and it was so eerie. Over seventy-five years' later, I still regard it as an extraordinary phenomenon and altogether quite an amusing one.

Most people who fly in an aircraft today are familiar with the sensation that is felt when an aircraft is suddenly caught in a strong downward air current, and drops like a stone. Our straps then have to hold us down so that we move in unison with the aircraft and do not rise up above our seats.

And sometimes an aircraft may rise in much the same way as a bird is swept upwards when it gets a free ride on an ascending convection current. Then we feel ourselves being pressed into our seats.

Such experiences may be fairly smooth in spite of the changes in altitude that they involve, which may be quite considerable. Over areas such as desert or generally barren terrain, heated air, becoming lighter, will often rise rapidly. The air may cool over open water, green fields or forest, becoming heavier and falling. Downward currents usually have slower vertical speeds than upward currents, but both can be smooth movements if there is no clashing with other, contrary, air movements.

Turbulence is another matter. That often happens when different air currents meet and mix, such as when cold air moves over a warm surface, or when, on a hot and humid day, an aircraft is caught in a cumulonimbus cloud, when it may be tossed about wildly (see Chapter 9).

In the 1970s, my wife Maureen and I flew over the Himalayas from Delhi to Srinagar in Kashmir and experienced the most turbulent conditions that we can remember. Weather-related air currents were caught up with those caused by a mass of rugged mountain peaks to maximise the turbulence. However, we were, of course, strapped in and were flying in an air-conditioned, pressurised modern aircraft. In such conditions, passengers may sometimes sleep undisturbed, often with little awareness of what is happening, even when the bumpiness is relatively violent, as it often is. (Turbulence is the most common cause of injury to air passengers, presumably because they are sometimes not strapped in at the appropriate time.)

It was totally different in a Second World War aircraft. In our Lancaster we were never strapped in; nor were other airmen.

The following was an experience that involved a considerable change in the aircraft's altitude but with no suggestion of turbulence.

On the night in question I was sitting at the navigator's desk in our Lancaster, and busy as usual. In front of me, my chart was spread out, and to the side of it were the accoutrements of my trade: dividers, a square protractor, several razor-sharp 2H and 4H pencils, a ruler, a sextant, the hand-held Dalton computer, a book of astronavigation tables, a planisphere and other essentials. I had just left my seat and moved to the astrodome to fix our position by the stars, calculated a new wind velocity (speed and direction) and had given the skipper a new course. I was entering the details in my log.

Suddenly, I found myself involuntarily detached from my seat, and then I rose, quite slowly and gently, above and away from my desk. The aircraft was obviously dropping through the air, and leaving me behind. After I had ascended about halfway towards the roof of the aircraft, there was a pause. I found myself dangling, as it were, in mid-air, and wondering what was going to happen next.

Powerful forces were controlling events and there was nothing I could do. Surprisingly, the pilot and flight engineer, who were only a short distance in front of me, saw nothing of my predicament and were unaware of the floating body just behind them. They were both, of course, busy, and they probably had also instinctively braced themselves to cope with the aircraft's movement.

Then my suspended but stationary state ended and I was once again propelled upward, still very smoothly, until I was pressed gently against the roof of the aircraft. There was no more scope for upward movement.

In those days, of course, I knew nothing of astronauts floating in space capsules, but today, seeing their relatively carefree demeanour while they float around, I think my experience must have been comparable, although they appear to have more control over their movements than I had. However, I was certainly not in the least concerned – just amazed at what had happened to me, and wondering what was going to happen next.

I looked down and could hardly believe the bare appearance of my desk. Usually fairly cluttered, it was now completely clear and hardly recognisable as my normal place of work. Since nothing on it had been fixed in position, that was hardly surprising, but at the time I wondered briefly what on earth had happened, in particular, to my chart, protractor, pencils and sextant.

In fact, they were not far away, on the same level as I was. Everything that was not pinned down in some way, including me, had risen, as the aircraft had dropped to a significantly lower altitude, but at a rate that had ensured my reasonable comfort throughout. All my equipment was also clinging to the roof, except for a couple of 2H pencils that were suspended a few inches away from my nose.

Today, when I turn over such events in my mind, I am still impressed by the amazing smoothness of my ascent. It was as if some unknown force had taken charge and was treating me with due consideration.

I don't know how long we (my tools of trade and I) were stuck up there. I remained reasonably relaxed – hopeful that before too long I would be back at my desk, as there was work to be done. Admittedly, I did not feel entirely comfortable about the prospect of my descent. Although I had risen gradually and gently, it was very possible that I would drop down rather more rapidly and unceremoniously, and perhaps land painfully – and where would that be? Perhaps on the hard, metal floor?

After some minutes, I sensed a change in the aircraft's movement and as I suddenly found myself separated from the roof, I prepared myself for a rapid and undignified descent. I was sure that our Lancaster was now about to rise vertically, and perhaps very rapidly, in a convection current. How fast would it rise? What would happen to me?

It is said that for every downward current there is a compensating rising current and as the former usually have slower vertical speeds than the latter, there was a probability that I would descend much faster than I had ascended.

But that wasn't the case. My wonderful luck continued. I floated downwards in a perfectly smooth and gentle way, exactly as I had ascended, except that there was no pause in my descent, until I was back in my seat. I could hardly believe the turn of events. It could all have been much more dramatic and much less comfortable.

Then, to my utter astonishment, I saw that my chart was in place along with all my bits and pieces. Everything kept on my desk had landed safely and in more or less the right place. There was no need for tidying or rearrangement. Again, it was as if some hidden force had taken charge of events. I suppose, in a way, it had. I still marvel at what happened: the absolutely smooth floatation, both up and down, and the return of all my equipment to more or less its previous position.

I suppose the whole incident had not lasted as long as it seemed but time was precious. After a few moments to consider what I had been engaged in before my 'float', and what was my next priority, I completed the log entries that had been interrupted, and then resumed the task of navigating. I selected three more stars to get another fix, worked out a new wind velocity and obtained another course for the skipper.

And what happened to the other crew members? I'm not entirely sure. Our rear gunner's tight little capsule left little scope for free upward movement and I imagine that the bomb aimer, mid-upper gunner, wireless operator and flight engineer all managed to brace themselves until the aircraft had settled down. None of the others, of course, had anything like all my loose equipment, nor did they have quite so much restraint-free scope for floating upwards.

Of course, we crew members did sometimes discuss, in leisure moments, various odd events experienced during our flights, but very often we didn't. Once on the ground, apart from debriefing, our minds were on food and relaxation – and why not? I never did find out what happened to everyone else on that occasion but I'm absolutely certain that no one else floated like an astronaut.

9

A MONSTROUS CUMULONIMBUS CLOUD!

Skip: 'Navigator, didn't I hear that we can expect some pretty rough weather tonight?'

Me: 'That's right, Skip. It's going to be very hot and humid all the way, and the Met people have warned us of widespread thunderstorms. You can see all around us that the cumulus clouds are billowing out quickly, so we should all keep a look out for cumulonimbus clouds.'

Skip: 'OK. You all heard that. Everyone keep a look out for whopping great clouds. Scotty [rear gunner] and Bill [mid-upper gunner] – you'll probably spot them first.'

Scotty: 'Actually, Skip, we've just passed one, about 5 miles or so to port: a huge black cloud, very low at the base. It had the usual anvil shape of a cumulonimbus at the top. There was also a lot of lightning around.'

Skip: 'There'll be more. Keep looking. I don't want us to go anywhere near them!'

Airmen make every effort to steer clear of cumulonimbus clouds. They are associated with thunder, lightning, and torrential rain or hail, violent convection currents, icing on the wings, interference to the electrical systems and sometimes tornadoes. Icing on the wings can be particularly dangerous because it adversely affects the aircraft's lift and therefore its ability to remain airborne.

Cumulonimbus (thunder) clouds can extend horizontally over 6 miles or more. The dark base, of water droplets, is often low, perhaps about 1,000 or 2,000ft above ground, while the vertical extent can tower to 40,000ft. There, the water droplets have become ice crystals, which form an anvil shape, caused by wind shear near the tropopause, the interface between the troposphere and the stratosphere.

The powerful, thermal air currents associated with cumulonimbus clouds can sweep an aircraft up 6,000ft, i.e. over a mile, at something like 100mph, or it can push it down at

A cumulonimbus cloud rising to a typical anvil shape. (Herbert Campbell/ Wikimedia Commons)

the same rate. While potentially dangerous, neither is necessarily life threatening. If, however, the aircraft flies between air currents moving in different directions, that can damage aircraft, and even cause small, light aircraft to break up.

When there is lightning, static electricity may build up in the airframe, which can interfere with the radio, disrupting electrical circuits and compass readings. Electrical storms can cause the aircraft to become an electrical conductor with the possibility of fire. A lightning strike on an aircraft can cause structural damage.

Between 10,000ft and 30,000ft especially, hail is fairly common in a cumulonimbus cloud. Hail consists of layers of ice, formed as the ice pellets move up and down in turbulent currents. A new layer of ice is formed every time the hail is raised high by convection currents. Eventually the pellets are heavy enough to overcome both air movements and gravity, and pound whatever lies below.

With cumulonimbus clouds there is often a rapid change of barometric pressure, which can affect the accuracy of altimeters.

Airspeed indicators have been known to ice up and give a false reading, which would be of great concern particularly to the pilot and navigator.

During the Second World War, if faced with cumulonimbus clouds, we navigators were required to carry out a simple procedure to keep our aircraft out of trouble. If one was spotted on the right (starboard), we would give the pilot the following course changes:

1. 60 degrees to port for three minutes;
2. 120 degrees to starboard for a further three minutes;
3. 60 degrees to port.

At 240mph that meant flying two legs, each of 12 miles, to complete two sides of an equilateral triangle, in order to bypass the cloud, before getting back on track.

If the cloud was on the port side, the equilateral triangle would, of course, be carried out on the right of our path:

1. 60 degrees to starboard for three minutes;
2. 120 degrees to port for three minutes;
3. 60 degrees to starboard.

That series of courses was intended to ensure that we gave a cumulonimbus cloud a wide berth, and it usually worked.

However, on one of our night flights, when we had to face a line of cumulonimbus clouds (associated with cold fronts and known as a squall line), it didn't.

Three of the clouds were circumvented quite successfully, in the way I've described, and then we faced a much larger one, which rose to an enormous height and was many miles in extent. Although it was night-time, there was light from those stars not obscured by clouds, and we had enough visibility to see the monster, especially as it was the source of extensive electrical activity. The lightning was spectacular.

Harmless cumulus clouds can grow into huge cumulonimbus ones only when the conditions are right: a mass of unstable air containing sufficient moisture, and heat. I think those conditions must have been optimal on this particular night.

It was our mid-upper gunner who first spotted the huge cloud that towered menacingly, mainly ahead, but a little to starboard. It was close enough for immediate concern, and our skipper took quick action to get away from it by flying to port. I followed that up by giving him the usual series of course changes, which he then carried out.

Unfortunately, the cloud was so extensive that when the bypass procedure had been completed we found that we had not evaded it completely but were still well within it. Our Lancaster was being pummelled by violent air currents, which threw it about wildly, while ice was spotted forming on the wings and threatening the aircraft's stability. The noise was deafening, especially when large hailstones began crashing down on our aircraft, which now seemed to be at the mercy of overwhelmingly powerful forces. It was a very dangerous situation and Skip's instinct was to get well away from it as soon as possible.

Incidentally, inside the Lancaster there was normally such a level of noise all the time that very little going on outside could be heard, including thunder, but when something hit the aircraft, including heavy rain or hail, it was very distinct.

This time the pilot asked me to give him a course – quickly. It seemed reasonable to assume that the main mass of the cloud was still to our starboard, so I gave him the first of the equilateral course changes given previously, followed by the others, but kept us on each leg for five minutes this time. So that each was 20 miles in extent.

I couldn't be certain that that would work as the extent of the cloud, which was evidently still growing outwards and upwards, could not be gauged. For much of the time that we were on the evasion courses, we were still caught in wildly unstable air movements, which seemed to be venting their fury on us, sucking us upwards and then dropping us like a stone, while the wings appeared to be wobbling alarmingly.

Finally our Lancaster seemed to be on an even keel, retaining its normal stable flight, and the cloud around us receded. It was suddenly wonderfully peaceful. An enormous relief.

It became clear, however, that the clouds were everywhere, so we all had to keep our eyes peeled. Fortunately, no other cumulonimbus clouds confronted us. The centre of the storm was now, we assumed, moving fairly rapidly away.

But we were not yet out of the woods. Following all those course changes, I needed to check exactly where we were. Skip had flown several miles in taking instinctive evasive action, and the constant changing of course gives scope for error.

In fact, I was fairly sure that we were well off track. I needed to fix our position quickly. A problem was that I needed an interval of good visibility for using my sextant, and since many cumulonimbus clouds were still in the area, the sky was now far from clear. Astronavigation is also hardly a quick process so the situation was of some concern.

However, after a few minutes of flying, I was able to identify a well-known star just before it was obscured by cloud. I sighted it in the bubble of my sextant, obtained a reading, consulted my air navigation tables and was able to plot one position line on my chart. Then I noticed another clearing, spotted another easily identified star and 'shot it'. Another position line was drawn. One to go.

I had to wait a little longer for the next opportunity as other cumulonimbus clouds lurked nearby, and at times the sky appeared almost totally covered with them, but finally I saw another familiar star and I quickly captured it in the bubble of my sextant, squeezed the trigger and obtained a precious altitude reading. With three position lines I was soon able to fix our position. We were indeed well off track.

However, I was now able to calculate a new wind speed and direction, and a new ground speed (speed over the earth's surface), and pass to our Skipper a new course. Happily that took us home without incident.

That night flight certainly involved a little extra excitement and we were all relieved when our base finally came into view. After all the noise and commotion caused by the storm – hailstones, wind, thunder, lightning and wing icing – the last few miles back to base seemed wonderfully quiet and peaceful.

10

REMARKABLE INCIDENTS REPORTED BY SOME OF OUR ACA MEMBERS

NORTH WEST ESSEX AND EAST HERTFORDSHIRE BRANCH

My own recollections, in the preceding chapters, of not-too-serious experiences, pale into insignificance when compared to some of the following examples of accidents, near accidents, and bizarre incidents, sometimes amusing, sometimes hazardous, taken from *Wings on the Whirlwind.* I have made only a small selection of happenings, which match the general character and scope of this book. Sadly, these former fellow members of our ACA branch are no longer with us.

★ ★ ★

Peter Kenworthy (102 and 216 Squadrons), a navigator, and fellow ACA member, has recalled a bombing raid when two crew members looked above their aircraft and became very agitated. Intrigued, Peter looked up too:

> I looked up straight into the bomb bay of the aircraft [above] and watched nine 1,000lb bombs come tumbling out of it. They passed between our starboard wing and our starboard tail plane, and inches [or so it seemed] from the fuselage.

He recognised the aircraft:

> Safely back home, I said to the captain of that aircraft: 'You dropped your bombs a bit close to us, Joe.' He said: 'Yes, I know. I thought I would have to go round again but my bomb aimer said, "It's OK, skipper, I can drop the bombs and miss them."'

Peter commented: 'Fortunately he had been right, but it would have been nice to have shared his confidence at the time.' (I think that was a very restrained observation.)

Sadly, there were several instances during the Second World War of bombs from one of our aircraft striking another one below. Sometimes such friendly fire must have destroyed the latter, though an aircraft holed by a bomb from another could sometimes remain airborne (see Chapter 13).

★ ★ ★

A Serious Incident – Especially in the RAF's View

The following was a not an uncommon happening at an Heavy Conversion Unit (HCU) where crews who had previously flown perhaps in two-engine Wellingtons converted to four-engine bombers such as the Lancaster or Stirling, which required the full length of the runway.

Returning from a routine training flight, the pilot left his descent too late and ran out of runway, or overshot (story told by George Smith [357 Squadron] the navigator). That was by no means a rare event in itself, but on this occasion there was a steamroller in the way, some yards beyond the end of the runway. The aircraft was a write-off (presumably so was the steamroller).

The very next day, the same crew were in another aircraft, and the pilot came in to land. Suddenly there was a terrible bang as a tyre burst. That might not have been too serious but this time there was a Halifax aircraft in the way as the aircraft settled on the grass to the side of the runway. So, following two days of flying when one aircraft had been written off and two severely damaged. George commented: 'It was one of those times when it was questioned, in no uncertain terms, whether we really were an asset to the RAF.'

However, George was later involved in a number of dangerous operations in the Far East (see below).

On Secret Operations

George Smith, like Tom Winup (discussed earlier), was involved on highly secret operations in Burma, French Indo-China (as it was), Thailand, Malaya (as it was) and Singapore, dropping and supplying agents, mainly British, American or Eurasian.

George's Liberator went on twenty-eight of these secret operations. Some of the flights were of astonishing length, one operation lasting for twenty-two and a half hours.

In order to carry enough fuel and still remain airworthy, the aircraft was stripped of armour plate, and both the number of guns and the amount of ammunition were reduced.

Three of the bomb bays were fitted with extra tanks so that about 1,000 tons of extra fuel could be carried. That grossly overloaded the aircraft, which became a flying petrol tank with little defence against a possible Japanese attack. The dangers were manifest, but in spite of the absence of reliable maps, and weather forecasts, the mission was successfully carried out. Every such operation was an extraordinary achievement. The public was never told about them.

Struggle with a Mae West in a Lancaster – Another Story in a Lighter Vein

Bill Porter (156 Squadron), a flight engineer, had an irritating mix-up with his Mae West, the inflatable life jacket under his webbing parachute harness, which was worn whenever an aircraft's flight involved flying over the sea. One day he was lifting heavy bundles of foil from behind the pilot's seat, to throw out of the 'chute in the bomb aimer's compartment. This was to jam German radar. Meanwhile, the pilot was corkscrewing the Lancaster to avoid a possible attack by German fighter planes flying nearby and posing a constant threat. With all that manoeuvring it was no easy task to deal with the silver foil.

Suddenly the inflating lever on the Mae West caught against something and it began to inflate under Bill's parachute harness.

He might have been able to deflate the Mae West, but he was a poor swimmer and was reluctant to be without it as they approached the North Sea. He might also have released his parachute harness, but that often offered the only chance of survival:

> I was gasping for breath as the Mae West and the parachute harness strangled me ... Fighter attacks could happen

anytime, so it wasn't advisable to strip off anything which contributed to your survival, even for a few minutes.

So Bill adopted a stooping posture to ease the pressure, at the risk of fellow crew members thinking that he had gone to sleep.

By the time his weary fellow crew members realised what had happened to Bill, their captain had successfully avoided the fighter attacks, and they were glad to release pent up tensions and have something to laugh about.

A Story Illustrating Some of the Risks Involved in the Bombing of Enemy Shipping

Eric Stone DFC (220 Squadron), a pilot, was involved in a very low-level attack on German shipping. On one particularly low-level bombing there was a very loud bang and the aircraft shuddered, but continued flying. When it had returned to base, it was discovered that part of a ship's mast was sticking out of the aircraft. As a member of the ground staff commented: 'You must have been pretty well on the deck!'

Eric was fortunate to survive that operation. Early in the war there was an air attack on the battleship *Admiral Scheer*, when the pilots were not so lucky.

A second wave of five Blenheims attacked the German battleship. The aircraft skimmed over the water on their approach and some pulled up just enough to clear the mast of the battleship while releasing their bombs. Only one Blenheim of the five returned from that operation. A German sailor who witnessed the attack spoke later of 'the reckless gallantry of the Blenheim crews'.

It is thought that in some cases the blast of the bombs when they exploded on the battleship destroyed the aircraft that had just released them but the *Admiral Scheer*

The German cruiser (pocket battleship) *Admiral Scheer* in port at Gibraltar c. 1936. There were Spanish Civil War neutrality, red, black and white stripes painted on her forward gun turret. (Official US Navy photo NH 59664/ Wikimedia Commons)

remained afloat. The Blenheim did not carry bombs with sufficient power to penetrate its armour.[1]

An Incident of Calm Impudence

Another of Eric Stone's recollections was when it was found that his aircraft, while on a bombing mission, was suddenly near a number of Junkers 88s. His aircraft happened to be the first to arrive near the target area and had not yet been spotted:

'Recognise those aircraft?' I asked the crew.
'Junkers 88s?' came the hesitant reply.
'Pretend we're one of them.' I said, 'We'll fly circuits with them. Switch on all navigation lights.'

They did so. The crew were all on tenterhooks.

> So good was our deception that we were even given a green
> light. Then we dropped our bombs from about 50ft and beat
> a hasty retreat. Not a shot was fired at us.

The Bravery of a Wireless Operator/Air Gunner

Eric Stone's aircraft flew over Brest noting the position of the
Scharnhorst and *Gneisenau*, two great German battleships.
There was fierce anti-aircraft fire and his Hudson sustained
some flak damage. Nevertheless, he managed to fly the
aircraft homewards without undue difficulty for nearly all
the way.

Then, suddenly, over Cardigan Bay, both engines stopped,
and the aircraft began gliding earthwards. He just made it
over the cliff top and crash-landed among the gorse bushes.
A Hudson could easily catch fire, so a rapid evacuation
took place.

'Come on! Get out! Quick!' he shouted, and the crew
rushed away as far as possible from the aircraft, expecting it
to catch fire, and perhaps explode, any minute. But one of
them was missing. Then they looked back. Eric explained:
'The WOP [wireless operator]/AG [air gunner] was standing
on the wing with a small fire extinguisher heroically pump-
ing little squirts on a smoking engine.'

An explosion could have occurred at any time.

A Courageous Attack on a U-boat

Douglas Thornton, a pilot from 500 Squadron, flew with
a New Zealander, Lloyd Trigg, about whom he recalled the
following:

Lloyd, while piloting a Liberator, attacked a U-boat, which fired back at him. His Liberator caught fire, but he pressed on, crashed on to the U-boat and sank it. Following the recommendation of the U-boat Commander, who was one of the first to be rescued, Lloyd Trigg was posthumously awarded the Victoria Cross.

That is an incredible story of bravery and also of an amazing involvement by the U-boat commander, without whose intervention no one would have known exactly what had taken place. I wanted to pursue this story, and have obtained the following supplementary information.

This attack on 11 August 1943 was Lloyd's first operational flight in a Liberator aircraft. The U-boat commander was Oberleutnant Klemens Schamong and his vessel was U-468. The attack was with depth charges. Evidently, the badly damaged U-boat sank soon after the attack with the loss of forty-two crew but seven survivors (including Schamong) were spotted by an RAF Sunderland of 204 Squadron in the dinghy of the crashed Liberator, drifting off the coast of West Africa. Rescued by HMS *Clakia*, Schamong reported the incident and recommended an award.

★ ★ ★

Derek Waterman DFC (96 and 158 Squadrons), a pilot – and our first ACA branch secretary – was returning from an attack on Duisberg, a large inland port on the Ruhr, Germany's great industrial area, known by the crews as 'the happy valley'. His Lancaster was named *Friday 13th*.

At 04.40 they received a disconcerting message to not return to Lissett, their base. They were told to land instead at Catfloss. The weather was perfect so the diversion had nothing to do with weather conditions.

They touched down at 05.15 and learned that there had been an accident to one crew when taking off for the raid. An engine had cut out during the take-off run. The pilot had already retracted his undercarriage. The aircraft, which slithered to a standstill just short of the boundary fence, and sustained some damage, was carrying 10,000lb of high explosives, which might well have immediately exploded.

The crew had lost no time in evacuating the aircraft.

An hour and a half after the crash the bombs had exploded, the aircraft being blown up into little pieces, which were scattered around the airfield, with jagged pieces all over the runway. It would not have been a good idea for any of the aircraft on operations to attempt a landing there on their return!

A Tragedy When Flying in Formation

Some pilots, perhaps otherwise entirely satisfactory, were not at all good at formation flying. Tom Winup, a bomb aimer (159 and 358 Squadrons), was once on a bombing leaders' course in Orissa, India:

Six of us were to fly in close formation on a fighter affiliation exercise with American Thunderbolts.

A New Zealander had a reputation for being the worst pilot in the world for keeping in formation. My first thought was: 'Right. I'm not flying with you, chum!'

However, I didn't have much choice and my aircraft's nose was right under the leading aircraft, which had our New Zealand friend as a co-pilot. It was Monsoon time and the weather was atrocious.

Suddenly, the aircraft to port hit the leader. With all four engines screaming, the New Zealander's aircraft, minus its tail unit, went down into a paddy field, whilst the other aircraft lost a wing, and also crashed. I was waiting for something to hit us, but a smart diving curve got us out of the way.

All the crew of the lead aircraft, including the New Zealander, were killed. In total, fourteen men were lost in this incident.

Not for the first time, Tom had had the closest shave imaginable.

The official account of the accident from the Ministry of Defence stated that:

At approximately 09.45 hrs, the formation approached a heavy bank of cloud. The leader, Sqn. Ldr. Heynert, commenced to lose height in an attempt to fly underneath this, but reached the cloud before he was quite low enough and the formation entered the cloud ...

Visibility was reduced to nil and numbers 2 and 5 in the formation altered course starboard. 4 altered course to port.

On coming out of the cloud ... aircraft 1 and aircraft 3 ... were seen to be in close proximity ... and 3 was then seen to collide with 1. The tail of 1 was torn off and the aircraft crashed out of control, and one wing of 3 was torn off, causing the aircraft to crash ... Neither pilot had the chance to execute a forced landing, nor was there sufficient time ... for a parachute descent.

★ ★ ★

Geoff King DFC (57 and 97 Squadrons), bomb aimer/navigator, recalls another horrific accident when carrying out a formation flying exercise:

We had just completed a small manoeuvre to port, when one Lancaster was caught in the slipstream of one of the leading aircraft above. He suddenly swept across above us, missing our aircraft by a few feet, then plunged over us again, and straight into the side of another aircraft. Both immediately started to disintegrate and dived into the fields north of Sleaford … We were all badly shaken up at seeing so many of our friends killed in this manner. There was only one survivor … thirteen airmen died.

First Trip to Berlin

Geoff describes what happened when, on 18 November 1943, his aircraft with over 400 others made its first trip to Berlin, the first of ten such flights:

Ahead of us lay what appeared to be an impenetrable screen of anti-aircraft fire … at all levels … As we neared our aiming point I concentrated on our bombing run and not on the hell that was going on outside the aircraft.

He 'instructed' the pilot: 'Bomb doors open. Left, left – steady, steady.'

I pressed the bomb release … and immediately the aircraft wanted to rise. 'Bomb doors closed.'

Below you could see some of the Halifaxes and Lancasters silhouetted against the inferno. I often wondered how many of the aircraft were hit by bombs from above …

It was just like a boiling cauldron below … I usually remained in the nose until we were clear of the target, keeping an extra eye open for fighters … There was a loss of nine aircraft … one of the lowest losses on this target.

Another Attack on Berlin

Bill Porter flew in a Lancaster to Berlin on 18 November 1943:

Buffeted around in the hail of ack-ack fire, and hearing the clang of shrapnel hitting old *P-Peter* [his Lancaster], I thought: 'We've had it now', but thanks to George, our skipper, jinking the Lanc around, we eventually got away.

They had reached Brandenburg, and soon they were over Berlin:

By this time the target was well alight. Our planes, silhouetted against this and the searchlights on the thick cloud beneath us, looked like strange insects crawling over a vast tabletop. We dropped our bombs and left.

Suddenly the pilot put the Lancaster into a steep nosedive:

There was a deafening roar and we plummeted like a broken lift. My feet left the floor … I felt sure that we would hit the ground.

Then George pulled *P-Peter* out of the dive but it had caused a casualty among the crew. The rear gunner had thought that the aircraft was going down for good. He had taken off his gloves to open his turret door to get his parachute for bailing out. Bill explained:

As he held on to the metal to pull himself out, his hands had been severely frost-bitten, and he had pulled all the skin off his palms and fingers … he remained on the rest bed, holding his painful hands in the air for the rest of the trip home.

When their Lancaster was nearly home, they had to take their place in the queue for landing but by that time their fuel gauges were showing almost empty. They were, nevertheless, instructed to carry on circling. The pilot then decided that he would be forced to jump the queue: 'We are short of petrol and we're coming in.'

They did so. The air gunner was taken to the RAF hospital in Ely.

Bill then looked at the damaged Lancaster with a ground crew sergeant. The side cowlings on both port engines had been ripped off, and the outer one had about 8ft of the flexible alloy air intake hanging down. The propeller tips on both were bent. Then there were nine flak holes in the fuselage between the two gunners. The astrodome had been sliced off. Another foot or so further forward and both the pilot and Bill would have been killed: 'It seemed that we had collided with two aircraft.'

The first one was struck as the Lancaster had to take sudden evasive action by going into a dive. The other aircraft took off the astrodome. During the dive, they hit another aircraft and sustained further damage.

Altogether this was certainly an evening of very close escapes and all the crew were lucky to be alive.

★ ★ ★

Geoff Cole DFC (103 and 241 Squadrons) was flying a Lancaster that was hit by a considerable amount of flak during a mission over Bochum in 1943. Nevertheless, he made the journey back to base successfully.

The next day the Parachute Section wanted to have a word with him. He was shown a black sticky mess hanging from a rack and told: 'This is your parachute Flight Lieutenant Cole.'

The parachute was one that was kept on seats, so that Geoff had been sitting on it.

Geoff said:

A piece of shrapnel had passed through the bomb doors, through a can of incendiary bombs, through the floor of the aircraft, through the bottom of my seat, and into my parachute. Being red hot it had melted the artificial silk into a burnt, glutinous mess ... had I not been wearing this type of parachute, I wouldn't be here to tell this story.

It's hard to imagine a closer escape than that. Geoff was later promoted to squadron leader.

NOTES

1 *Bomber Command*, page 8

11

AT 28,000FT, I ROLLED OFF THE WING OF MY MOSQUITO

THE INCREDIBLE STORY OF GEORGE CASH DFC 139 & 571 SQUADRONS AND 1409 METEOROLOGICAL FLIGHT, MEMBER OF THE 'CATERPILLAR CLUB'

It was in *Wings on the Whirlwind* that I first read about the amazing experiences of George Cash, which marked the final instalment of his time as a navigator in the RAF during the Second World War. Later, I had a few words with George about those events during one of our monthly lunches of the ACA (North West Essex and East Hertfordshire branch) at The Chequers in the village of Ugley, near Quendon in Essex.

George flew in Mosquitos, which had a crew of two, so he did everything that the pilot was unable to do, including navigating, machine-gunning, bomb-aiming and operating the wireless.

De Havilland Mosquito B.XVIs, including the Percival-built PF563 (closest to the camera). This twin-engine aircraft was a very effective, high-speed, high-altitude, multi-role combat aircraft that was made almost entirely of wood. Its crew consisted of only a pilot and a navigator. Mosquitos proved to be ideal for attacks on pinpoint targets such as railways and factories. Later in the war they were often used as pathfinders, lighting with flares the target area for the main bombing force. (Royal Air Force/Wikimedia Commons)

His aircraft had been on operations for nearly a year and the events outlined below occurred on Tuesday, 18 July 1944. His pilot was S/L Terry Dodwell, known as 'Doddy'.

There was a last minute change of plan. Instead of an operation over Cologne, his aircraft was switched to Berlin. This was because Doddy felt that they were replacing a sprog crew that were not yet ready for the challenges of Berlin.

When Doddy tested the engines, he found that the port one was unserviceable. That meant that they had to use a spare Mosquito. Consequently, their take-off was delayed and they were fifteen minutes behind the other aircraft. They couldn't possibly catch up with them and would be alone approaching the target, and therefore very vulnerable to attack from both anti-aircraft fire and night fighters.

Their fears were realised well before they reached the target area, the railway marshalling yards near Berlin. They were flying at their operational height of 28,000ft near Wittingen when they were attacked. Shells began to burst around the Mosquito and Doddy responded very quickly, climbing the aircraft as high and as fast as possible. However, a huge lump of shrapnel smashed through a window and into the Gee (radar) box only a few inches from George, his first very narrow escape from death during this operation.

They pressed on and arrived over Stendal, their last turning point.

Suddenly they were coned by searchlights and blinded by the glare. Doddy responded by diving, banking, turning and climbing in an effort to escape but to no avail. They were still the focus of the searchlights. Then the searchlights dipped: an ominous sign. Night fighters were about to attack. Ahead they could see the target indicators and George noted in his log: '02.00 hours. Target sighted. Preparing to bomb.'

George now knelt down and prepared to crawl into the nose of the aircraft, to the bomb sight. But he had no time to do so, as:

> … we felt a quick succession of bumps as cannon shells smashed into the fuselage. A tremendous 'whoof' was heard and the petrol tank exploded. The port engine burst into flames.

The cockpit was now fully ablaze and the aircraft on the verge of complete destruction. It had all happened in a matter of seconds. Doddy shouted: 'Come on. We've got to get out of here!'

It was no longer possible to use the usual exit below the navigator's position so Doddy, whose seat was now ablaze, exited through the top one. This was highly dangerous since there was a considerable risk of being struck by the tail fin and rudder. (Sadly, as George discovered later, Doddy was probably hit and did not have the chance to use his parachute.)

The aircraft was now filled with flames and smoke, and spiralling out of control with a 4,000lb bomb on board. In such a desperate situation there seemed to be little hope that George would survive for long:

> Despite the heat in the cockpit and my perilous position, a calmness came over me and my mind was clear. A fierce draught fanned the flames so that the whole cockpit was ablaze and full of smoke. There was nothing for it – I had to go out of the top hatch.

As George prepared to go, his elbow caught the ruined Gee box. The parachute was knocked from his hand, and fell down the escape hatch – but it stuck halfway. He grabbed it and clipped it on to his harness:

> Suddenly I remembered reading an account in *Tee Emm* about how a Mosquito navigator had bailed out by climbing out of the top hatch and rolling on to the starboard wing before letting go.

George took time to take three deep breaths of oxygen, then threw off his oxygen mask and helmet and made his way through the flames, to the top exit. Once through it, and clutching grimly the edges of the wing to avoid being blown away by the fierce slipstream, George succeeded in rolling on the wing a sufficient distance to keep him clear of the tailplane. He then let himself go, and the slipstream carried him away.

After dropping, he counted 'One, two, three', reached up to his parachute and pulled the release handle. Nothing happened. He continued to fall. He had to try again: 'I then reached up with both hands, and pulled open the flaps of the pack. There was then a plop as the canopy sprang out and filled with air. Then I was floating through the quiet, peaceful sky.'

Looking below him, George saw his Mosquito blazing in a field: 'The "cookie" was still on board. If it had gone up then, I would have gone up with it. I continued drifting a little way away. Then suddenly, innumerable fingers were scrabbling at me.'

The 'fingers' were, in fact, twigs. George had fallen into a tree. In the blackness of the night, he couldn't see anything, including the ground below. But feeling that he had to get down, he pressed the release button of his parachute, and fell 10ft or so – into a bush.

Many years later George reflected on that part of his story:

I am one of the very few men who bailed out from the top of a Mosquito and lived to tell the tale. Also, I am one, probably of many, who got down from a tree that he had not climbed up!

After two days of walking, and passing through a small village near Magdeburg very late at night, George was captured and became a prisoner of war on 1 August 1944, in Stalag Luft I, on his twenty-third birthday. He spent ten months there.

Then he made a fascinating discovery. While playing bridge with a fellow prisoner, and exchanging recent histories, he discovered that his companion was a Flight Lieutenant Thompson, also of 571 (George's) Squadron, who had been shot down on his first operation. He was, in fact, the pilot with whom Doddy had switched operations. However, Thompson and his navigator had been taken off the battle order and put down as a reserve crew. It was two days later that that they were shot down over Hamburg, when his navigator had been killed.

Many years after the war, George discovered more about the shooting down of his aircraft, and another strange twist to his story: 'Apparently we had been tracked and shot down by a German night fighter ace – Oberleutnant Heinz Struning … flying a Heinkel 219A-5.'

The Heinkel was armed with upward firing guns and its engines were fitted with nitrous oxide boosters, which could be used for about ten minutes to enhance their speed.

'Heinz Struning was awarded the Oak Leaves to his Knight's Cross with Swords and Diamonds for shooting us down,' commented George.

Further research about the German night fighter ace, who had been promoted to Hauptmann following his success, unearthed a remarkable coincidence. On Christmas Eve 1944, Struning's aircraft was shot down by a Mosquito night fighter and crashed. His radio operator and air gunner bailed out safely, but the tail of the Messerschmitt 110 hit Struning when he bailed out, and he was killed.

To sum up, a Mosquito pilot – Doddy – was killed when bailing out of a Mosquito that had been fatally damaged by the attack of a Heinkel, piloted by Herr Struning. Subsequently, a Mosquito shot down Struning's Messerschmitt, and he was killed while bailing out. Both pilots were killed when struck by the tailplane of their own aircraft. As George commented: 'Truth can be stranger than fiction!'

George Cash completed thirty-six operational flights and was awarded the DFC. The *London Gazette* of 18 August 1944 included these words: 'At all times his skilful navigation and his determination to cover the route ordered have contributed largely to the success of these missions.'

12

THE LONG MARCH TO FREEDOM

I had survived being shot down and near fatally wounded; I had survived prison camps; I had survived weeks of marching in atrocious weather; I had survived hunger and thirst.

The words of Douglas Fry that sum up his ordeals

Douglas was an air gunner with 15 Squadron, 3 Group, flying in a Stirling, and on the night of 30–31 July 1943 their target was Remscheid. Over the target area, the Stirling was coned by searchlights, and anti-aircraft guns managed to get their range. The aircraft was hit by the first salvo. They nevertheless continued with their bombing run, and, in spite of the heavy flak, dropped their bombs on the selected targets.

Soon afterwards, however, a fire on the port side of the fuselage began to spread alarmingly. Douglas left his turret and went to try to put out the fire, but just then a shell burst nearby and a piece of shrapnel hit him in the stomach. The Stirling then received a direct hit that sent it into a

Three Stirling bombers taking off in Great Britain, April 1942. The Stirling was the first four-engine bomber and was used for a limited period, until higher performance aircraft such as the Lancaster and Halifax became available. It was used for mining ports, and as a glider during the allied invasion in 1944. (Library of Congress)

steep dive and Douglas found himself pinned to the roof of the fuselage.

The pilot, although by now badly wounded, managed to pull the aircraft out of the dive, but it would not remain airborne for much longer. It was time to bail out, but Douglas found that his parachute had broken loose from its rack and had disappeared. He looked around, found it, clipped it on, and bailed out of the rear escape hatch.

Of the seven crew members, four – who had still been aboard when Douglas bailed out – died. The flight engineer and rear gunner had abandoned the aircraft earlier. In Douglas' words:

My parachute opened almost as soon as I had left the aircraft, which was flying away with flames streaming from her
– and four of my crew still on board. I think I bailed out at
about 5,000ft. It was a clear night and I was just able to see
the ground coming up to meet me. It was then that I realised
that I was drifting towards a wall. I just managed to avoid it
by lifting my feet at the last moment.

Having landed in a garden, and feeling increasingly weak
from his wounds, Douglas managed to release his parachute
harness and take off his life jacket before passing out.
He was given some help by a German family, who protested
successfully when a large German in a black uniform arrived
and wanted to shoot him.

After being moved about, and falling in and out of consciousness, Douglas was finally operated on by a Polish
doctor (also a prisoner) and was later sent to Stalag Luft V1,
a POW camp at Heydekrug in East Prussia (as it was), and
soon settled down to its spartan, often very uncomfortable life. He was very appreciative of the Red Cross parcels,
which arrived from time to time, because the food provided
by the Germans was meagre. Occasionally, to his joy, a letter
arrived from home and sometime later a parcel arrived containing such welcome articles as a sweater, a toothbrush,
some dentifrice, socks, handkerchiefs and soap, but the
pyjamas that had been listed had been stolen.

The East Prussian winter was very severe and it was a
great relief when spring came and the POWs were able to
go outside more often.

From 6 June 1944 (D-Day) onwards, however, there
was increasing confusion, as, with the Russians approaching from the East, refugees moving ahead of the Russian
advance, and more news of the Allies advancing from the

West, the Germans seemed progressively more anxious to prevent their POWs from being rescued.

Eventually, Douglas and about 800 other POWs were sent on a journey in a very dirty cattle truck to the port of Memel. That was followed by three days and nights in the filthy hold of a ship, where there was no available floor space for sleeping and no toilet facilities (a bucket was lowered on a rope for that purpose). Down there, Douglas spent three days and three nights squatting on a girder. That was followed by another journey in a cattle truck from Swinemünde to Kiefheide.

After a march, they arrived at Stalag Luft IV, at Grosse-tychow, where they heard some disturbing news:

> … the men in the first column had been manacled in twos and forced to run up the road at bayonet point, the Luftwaffe guards having been reinforced by a bunch of young thugs from the Kriegsmarine. They were very free with their bayonets and stabbed several chaps or frequently hit them with their rifle butts. The German guard dogs bit other men, and all the time the Germans were screaming abuse … We were kept hanging around outside the camp nearly all day without any food or drink … Eventually, after protest, a bucket of water was passed around.

The POWs slept on bare boards in little huts, described as 'like big dog kennels', in which they could not stand up. Douglas recalls: 'There was an air of foreboding over the camp and a sense of impending disaster. The doom-laden atmosphere was not helped by the scarcity of food.'

During a very violent storm, one of the 'dog kennels' was struck by lightning and it was like a bomb exploding. Several POWs were struck by the blast and one, a pilot, was killed: 'The Third Reich was falling apart, and in spite of Allied successes everywhere, our future was becoming increasingly uncertain.'

They were eventually moved into a new, but unfinished compound, with no lighting or stoves. Food was still scarce, although occasionally a Red Cross parcel arrived – one between two.

On 6 February, after being woken up at about 5 a.m. and then kept standing outside in freezing conditions, at 8.30 a.m. they began their long march. There was snow on the ground and blizzard conditions.

They had all tried to prepare for this inevitable next step, but were ill equipped for the awful conditions. They had been given Red Cross parcels at the last minute with no time to pack them away, so some items had to be discarded:

> It was snowing and the going was heavy. The roads were inches deep in snow and ice so that it was difficult to keep on one's feet. The guard in charge of our particular column lost his way. There we were, traipsing around in pitch darkness, in alternating rain and snow, looking for the farm where we were supposed to sleep that night.

Eventually, their destination was located, and Douglas, soaking wet, hungry and desperately cold, noted that hundreds of POWs had arrived earlier and taken up all the floor space, so he flopped down in the darkness in a hayloft, unaware that he was on the very edge of a gaping hole 10ft above the floor.

The next day the march continued in atrocious weather, and again little or no food was made available but they were saved by the occasional Red Cross parcels, which had been placed as far as possible at strategic places along the route of the march.

When passing through a village '… some little old ladies dressed in black, peasant-type garb, came out of their front doors and put buckets of water by their gates so that we could grab a drink as we went past'.

However, the guards who were leading the POW march kicked over the buckets so the kind action of the ladies was to no avail.

They continued marching and the foul weather was unchanged. Douglas's hands were so numb that he was unable to open his pack to see whether there was any food left there:

> … my hands were so cold that I could not unfasten it. I gave up, leaned back to rest my weary body, and promptly fell asleep. If I had not been awakened, or for some reason had been left lying there, I would have frozen to death in my sleep.

On around 15 February, after completing a march of about 120 miles, they arrived at a place called Pritter, where in spite of the awful weather, they had to sleep in the open. By the morning they were covered in frost. As they moved off the next morning, Red Cross food parcels were distributed, one between two. They marched to Swinemünde, where a ferry took them to Usedom. From there they continued marching for several days:

> The weather was still wet and raw and we were, as usual, hungry. We had not received a bread ration, nor any thing else, and our last issue of Red Cross food had long been eaten. As usual, we milled about in the mud, trying to keep warm, and trying not to think of food, although always hoping that something would turn up.

Several more weeks of marching and sleeping in the open or in barns followed and still they were given very little to eat. They crossed the River Elbe at Dömitz.

At Ebsdorf they were again transported in filthy cattle trucks and then they slept on the ground of a large marquee in Fallingbostel, where they received Red Cross parcels, one between two. The only food they received from the Germans was thin, greasy soup with a few pieces of turnip floating in it:

> After eleven days in this awful place, we were ordered to march again, this time eastwards, as the British army was advancing rapidly towards us, and the Germans would not let us stay in one place to be rescued. They were treating us as hostages.

Douglas was resting in a village when he noticed a heavily pregnant young woman who was eyeing his flying sweater enviously:

> My chum, Danny Heath, and I had no food and so I thought I would try a bit of bargaining. I asked the woman if she could get me a loaf of bread in exchange for my sweater … She made signs that she would unravel the wool and make clothes for her baby … I obtained a huge freshly baked, 3 kilo loaf … Danny and I could now eat.

On 17 April they crossed the Elbe on a large raft. At Camin, they slept in a barn, which alongside other buildings was bombed. The barn, full of straw, was soon alight. It was quickly abandoned. Some POWs were killed in the bombing, including two on either side of Douglas, and others were seriously injured. Douglas received a small shell splinter in his back.

The wounded survivors were taken by horse-drawn cart to a small POW camp near Schwerin where they were treated in the sick bay, which was staffed by POWs.

After ten more days, on 2 May, the guards suddenly disappeared. The prisoners were free but surrounded by a chaotic situation with refugees passing through in large numbers, and the arrival of wounded German soldiers, including some deserters, as well as Russians, who had also been POWs. Some of the latter took their revenge on any Germans they met.

Finally some Americans arrived with welcome rations for the British POWs and four days later they were all taken to Lüneburg and billeted in some German barracks, where they were well fed until the time came for them to fly back to England:

> We had a good flight back and landed at an airfield in the Midlands. As we got out of the Lancaster, there were WAAFs waiting who welcomed us home and even as I recount these events my heart goes out to these lovely ladies who led us to a hangar decked out with bunting. There were tables laid with tea, cakes and sandwiches. A small RAF dance band was playing and WAAFs invited us to dance. The whole welcome was quite overwhelming.

Looking back over his experiences, Douglas observed that when his taxi arrived at his house:

> There was bunting and a banner across the front of the house, with the words WELCOME HOME. There was also a huge key hanging on the door in celebration of my 21st birthday, which had been on May 3rd, the day after I was liberated by our American friends. My mother was waiting anxiously at the top of the steps …

I have included above what I hope is the essence of George Cash's and Douglas Fry's experiences because I found them both moving examples of courage and fortitude and believe they should have a wide circulation. George passed away a few years ago, in his mid 90s; both Douglas and his wife died more recently.

13

A VERY SPECIAL SKIPPER

SQUADRON LEADER GERALD (GERRY) DE LUCIE CARVER DSO DFC, PILOT WITH 37 AND 78 SQUADRONS

Gerald Carver was awarded his pilot's brevet in March 1941. That's always a moment of joy and immense satisfaction. Perhaps, however, in the following months, everything did not go entirely smoothly with Gerry's RAF career. Firstly, his Operational Training Unit (OTU) instructor decided that 'he was inclined to be lazy, could have done better', and then his Link Trainer instructor assessed him as 'below average'.

The truth is that Gerry, who rose to be a deservedly well-decorated squadron leader, was modest, courageous, highly skilled and an outstanding leader, as the following five accounts (and others could be related) illustrate.

Portrait of Gerry as a flight
lieutenant.

While most of these Wellingtons are in a fairly close formation, two appear
to have been assigned a special role. (I am grateful to James Morley for
permission to use this excellent photograph)

★ ★ ★

Gerald was involved in a night attack in Wellingtons on a German fighter base in Derna, Libya.

The weather was poor, and as the cloud base was 4,000ft they had to attack lower than planned. Accurate flak was encountered, and the starboard engine was hit and put out of action, but the bombing was successfully carried out. The aircraft turned towards base, which involved flying close to the coast.

However, as the Wellington flies with difficulty on only one engine, all surplus equipment had to be jettisoned. Progress was still very slow and uncertain, and it became clear that they were not going to make it. It was eventually decided that there was no reasonable alternative but to ditch, in the blackness of night, in the sea.

The landing, or ditching, in the sea was inevitably a very rough one, but the Wellington did not sink immediately, and all the crew managed to leave the aircraft and enter the water. However, to their dismay, the dinghy broke loose and drifted away. Four of the crew managed to reach it and clambered in but the wireless operator/gunner and navigator were carried away by the strong current. Flares and rockets were used to try to guide them, but there was no response. Then Gerald made his own rescue attempt:

> … attached by a rope, I swam round the dinghy to try to locate and rescue them, but to no avail. Eventually we lost all contact and it became strangely quiet … A horrible silence fell over the four of us in the dinghy when no more voices came to us from the darkness. We were very despondent.

The survivors assessed their injuries: one broken rib, one dislocated shoulder and various cuts and bruises. They had no serious injuries but all four were by now exhausted and ill equipped to paddle the dinghy, while a strong current kept them out at sea when they were striving to reach the shore. It took them three hours to beach the dinghy. The enemy were nearby so they had to act quickly: 'I managed to secrete the three crew members in a disused pill box and set out to get help.'

Gerald trekked through the desert. He had no idea how long it would take before he could get help. Fortunately, after about two hours, he was able to hitch a lift on an army lorry. That was very useful but only took him part of the way to the kind of help he needed – a vehicle at his disposal and medical assistance.

Finally, however, Gerry was able to make contact with a British medical centre, and he returned to the pillbox with an ambulance to rescue the three crew members. They had been incarcerated for ten hours, presumably with little or no food or water. Unsurprisingly, all four needed to spend three days in hospital before returning to their base.

This is a sad story but also one of outstanding bravery and great leadership, without which none of the crew would have survived.

* * *

On a raid over Berlin in August 1943 there were many aircraft over the target area. Several, coned by searchlights, were intent on evading anti-aircraft fire while others were being attacked by enemy night fighters. Yet others, also under fire, had started their bombing run, with the pilots striving to keep the aircraft steady, and follow the precise instructions of their bomb aimers, perhaps in spite of a buffeting by the slipstream of another aircraft a little ahead. The dangers were many. Apart from the bullets, cannon fire, and shrapnel from anti-aircraft fire, there was debris from destroyed aircraft dropping on aircraft just below them, and also bombs falling from above, sometimes from aircraft belonging to the same squadron. And all around there was blinding light and the rattling of shrapnel on metal.

In other words, it was a fairly typical raid on Berlin or the Ruhr.

Gerry was piloting one of the many Lancasters involved in the raid and he was carefully following his bomb aimer's guidance on the bombing run when another aircraft, which was also just above the target area, released its bombs, one of which punched a hole through his port wing, narrowly missing the starboard engine and a petrol tank. It was thought to be a 500lb bomb.

Passing right through the wing, the bomb had made a large hole with an ugly, twisted tear, which made it difficult to keep the aircraft steady while reducing its lift. Yet the Lancaster, expertly handled, remained airborne, though Gerry may have found it less manoeuvrable and therefore less able to evade night fighter attacks.

However, he was determined to complete his task: 'We pressed on and managed to get back on track and complete our bombing run without further mishap.'

The damaged aircraft was now very vulnerable, with several night fighters in the area.

We experienced a number of combats and a few near misses with enemy fighters. Our rear gunner shot down one Messerschmitt 109, which was confirmed, and another unconfirmed. Other fighters with which we had a brush were a Messerschmitt 110 and a Junkers 88.

Finally, Gerry was able to get clear of the danger zone and head for home and his base in eastern England.

Over the airfield, with doubts about the extent of damage, apart from the wing, a safe landing could not be certain, but Gerry, with the skill that he demonstrated on other occasions (see below), brought down his Lancaster without undue difficulty – a truly great achievement.

★ ★ ★

Three months later, Gerald was involved in another very dangerous event in his Lancaster. During a raid over Ludwigshafen his crew encountered a heavy burst of flak. Shrapnel damaged the hydraulics and the bomb-release mechanism. Every effort was made to release the bombs, including weaving, diving and corkscrewing the aircraft, but all to no avail. They had to return to base carrying the bombs. Gerald said, 'The slightest jolt on landing could blow us to kingdom come.'

One can imagine the tension among the crew as Gerald brought his damaged, bomb-laden aircraft nearer to the runway. But he used all his skill to save both his crew and his aircraft, making a very special effort to avoid a catastrophe: 'I made the smoothest landing in my entire flying career!'

Attack on Peenemünde

Everyone living in Britain at the time will remember the doodle bugs (V1s), which were flying bombs that flew over Britain in 1943–44, and afterwards the V2 rocket-propelled bombs that, unlike the former, were silent killers that rained death and destruction on our cities. As Hitler's armies were being forced back on both Western (Allied) and Eastern

(Russian) fronts, he placed increasing dependence on such weapons to reverse his fortunes.

On 17 August 1943, Gerald took part in a raid, with 600 other aircraft, mainly Lancasters, on Peenemünde, an island in the mouth of the River Oder, where the rockets were designed and developed under the direction of Dr Wernher von Braun. Gerald tells the story of the raid:

It was arguably the most important Bomber Command raid of the war ... High security surrounded the raid ... It was cleverly planned with diversionary Mosquito attacks on Berlin to coincide with the time of the main attack ... The results were successful as bombs were concentrated in the development and production areas of the site, as was proved from subsequent photographic reconnaissance.

The losses were forty-one aircraft. We experienced some light flak from flak ships. A smoke screen was employed to try to obscure the target but it was not very effective.

I had a feeling of having really achieved something for the war effort ... German plans were set back by about nine months.

We now know that the diversionary attack certainly was successful in so far as the first wave of Lancasters over Peenemünde met few night fighters, the majority of them being concentrated around Berlin where the main attack was expected.

By the time of the second wave, however, the Germans were alerted to the purpose of the Mosquito attack, and had redirected all available night fighters to the area being attacked.

★ ★ ★

Gerry's Potato Patch

Unwelcome, sometimes life-threatening, developments could occur at the very beginning of a flight. When taking off in his Lancaster for an operation to bomb a munitions factory in France, and with his aircraft still gathering speed on the runway, Gerald discovered that the Air Speed Indicator was not registering. He needed an accurate measurement of speed to ensure that his Lancaster was fast enough to climb, especially with a full bomb load.

He therefore tried everything in an attempt to abort the take-off, but the aircraft ran off the end of the runway, crashed through the perimeter fence and then ploughed into a field of potatoes.

Much leg-pulling followed. The field was henceforth known as 'Gerry's potato patch'. Gerry's response was: 'Well, at least we haven't had our chips!' i.e. we survived!

14

DEATH WAS NEVER FAR AWAY

Flight Lieutenant Clifford Storr, a member of 100 and then 103 Squadron, was a navigator in a Lancaster. He was one of that rare few who managed to survive about fifty operations in two tours, over enemy territory. It was not possible to do that without experiencing several brushes with death, and, as any experienced airmen will attest, without also having a generous amount of luck.

Eight of Cliff's operations were over Berlin, when his aircraft was frequently coned by searchlights and came under heavy anti-aircraft fire; after that, night fighters would often attack. On each occasion, the Lancaster returned home safely, albeit sometimes with relatively minor damage.

Probably his worst experience was when his Lancaster was attacking targets in the Leipzig area, when seventy-nine aircraft were shot down. If they were all Lancasters, which have a crew of seven, that would have meant the loss of 553 airmen, but no doubt a proportion of them managed to bail out successfully and become POWs.

An outstanding photograph from the Shuttleworth Military Pageant of Britain's only surviving flying Lancaster. The Lancaster was Britain's most successful heavy bomber and its performance and tolerance under attack were much appreciated by all aircrews. (Contributed with grateful thanks by Tim Felce)

On 14 January 1944, the attack was in the Brunswick area. The specific target was identified, the bomb aimer took charge on the bombing run, and the operation was successfully carried out.

Cliff then gave the pilot the course to take them home and the Lancaster began the homeward flight.

So far the crew had been lucky, but they knew, from incidents during past operations, that they could be attacked at any time until they were safely across the Channel. The air gunners especially remained vigilant, but it was the wireless operator who spotted an enemy aircraft, though, oddly enough, it did not appear to be about to attack them.

They had been homeward bound for only a few minutes when he looked through the astrodome and reported that a Junkers 88 was flying above them. There followed a hurried, uncertain conversation:

Pilot: 'In which direction is it flying?'

W/OP: 'It's flying in the same direction as us, and seems to be maintaining its distance from us.'

Pilot: 'That's a bit odd. Anyway, if it stays up there it won't threaten us, but keep a close eye on it.'

Unfortunately, this may not have been good judgement, as events suggested. Suddenly one of the crew of the Junkers 88 shot down a red flare, which landed squarely on the Lancaster and made it an illuminated sitting duck. Almost immediately afterwards another Junkers 88 appeared and began intensive firing with all its guns. Cliff Storr watched in horror as tracer bullets whistled through the Lancaster. One minute their aircraft had been progressing steadily and peacefully on its homeward-bound journey, and the next, as one crew member put it, 'all hell was let loose'.

The pilot, knowing that his aircraft was already badly damaged, reacted quickly, lowering its nose and putting it into a very steep dive in an effort to escape complete destruction. The Lancaster was screaming as it dived towards the ground, pursued by at least two Junkers 88s.

Cliff could not see how they could escape and still, at 93, remembered the thoughts that rushed through his head, including: 'I am about to die.'

He says that oddly enough he recalls no fear of dying but he was angry at the thought that he had had no chance to do anything in life. He was about to be robbed of his future.

The pilot seems to have shared Cliff's thoughts about the hopelessness of their situation for he shouted to the crew: 'Bail out if you can!'

Cliff reached under his working desk where he kept his parachute. It may have been partly a result of the tossing and turning of the Lancaster as the pilot strove to evade its pursuers, but at that point something very unfortunate occurred. He accidentally pulled the ripcord and the parachute billowed out in the aircraft. He was horrified. His opportunity to bail out had disappeared. Whatever happened next he would have to remain in the Lancaster. He was resigned to what appeared to be the inevitable. He was helpless and the aircraft was still under attack.

Suddenly, good fortune intervened. The Lancaster entered a wide expanse of cloud and was immediately out of sight of the enemy aircraft. The hail of bullets ceased abruptly, and it was suddenly eerily quiet except for the Lancaster's four noisy Merlin engines. No member of the crew had bailed out.

The pilot held his course for some minutes and then dared to turn the aircraft on to the course that Cliff had given him. They were homeward bound once again, though not at all sure that their battered Lancaster would remain airborne for long. Some of its damage was visible but they all knew that there had probably been some serious damage that they could not see, but which had not yet affected the Lancaster's response to the controls. And perhaps the Junkers 88s would suddenly appear and attack them again, to finish them off.

Miraculously, their Lancaster did manage to limp home, there were no further attacks, and it was soon above its base. A critical juncture had now been reached. The crew would soon learn the worst about the Lancaster's damage. They were not at all sure what would happen next. Would they be able to get down safely? Was there any chance of a landing? They hadn't long to wait.

Control told them that the extent of their damage could be clearly seen. It was, as feared, widespread. In particular, they noted: 'You have only one leg down [undercarriage]. Landing will be very dangerous. Whether or not you attempt it is up to you.'

The pilot then said to his crew:

Control thinks that landing the kite will be highly dangerous.
I think you'll stand a better chance if you bail out. I'm afraid
Cliff can't, as he doesn't have a parachute. He and I will have
to take our chance.

The response of the other crew members was unanimous. They were not going to leave the aircraft for the pilot and Cliff to face alone the hazards expected in attempting to land. They would all stay together.

There could be only a crash landing and it would certainly be an extremely risky one, in view of the Lancaster's damage, especially as that included a broken undercarriage.

The pilot dipped the nose of the Lancaster and approached the runway while all the crew took up crash positions. They all knew that the aircraft might break up and/or catch fire as it crashed on the tarmac.

Neither of those results happened, but the crash landing was accompanied by a succession of deafening sounds. As soon as the one wheel touched the runway, the wing on the opposite side, quite unsupported, crashed down on to the tarmac, with a loud and ugly scraping noise, giving all the crew a terrifying shock. The aircraft then skidded, scraped and screamed its way off the runway, completely out of control, crashed through a barrier and eventually came to rest in a pond. It was now a complete write-off.

There was silence for a few moments, almost as if no one had survived. Then the crew, with a variety of injuries, none of them life threatening, slowly crawled out of their mangled aircraft – all except for the rear gunner. Sadly he had died, a casualty of the crash landing. The other members of the crew would soon fly again, on yet another sortie, with another rear gunner.

A sequel to this story is that the next day, Cliff received a note from the Parachute Section. Whether or not it was intended as a joke is not clear. It requested payment of two shillings and sixpence (half a crown or thirty old pence) in view of the condition of the parachute that Cliff had returned! As Cliff says, that was a lot of money in those days. He paid up anyway. He thought it best to stay on good terms with those who prepared the parachutes so carefully for every operation.

★ ★ ★

Cliff has related incidents during two of his Lancaster's eight attacks on targets in the area of Berlin.

On the first of these, his navigation seems to have been particularly successful, so much so that their Lancaster was over the target well ahead of every other aircraft involved in the raid.

The inevitable consequence was that they were coned by dozens of searchlights. They were alone in the sky and the focus of attention. All the crew braced themselves for a fierce onslaught of concentrated anti-aircraft fire. As Cliff put it: 'We thought we would be blasted out of the sky.'

But it didn't happen. For reasons unknown, the gunners below appeared to hesitate, as if they were not at all sure about the origin of the lone aircraft, 20,000ft above their heads. Cliff then told the crew about a point made by the intelligence officer.

He said that there was a possibility that the German colours of the day for friendly aircraft would be red and yellow: 'We could fire some red and yellow flares.'

Pilot: 'It's worth a try. Wireless operator, have you got some red and yellow flares?'

Wireless operator: 'Yes, skip, I've got them ready.'

Pilot: 'Good. Fire them and we'll see what happens.'

The wireless operator did so and the crew, each one no doubt holding his breath, waited …

It worked. After a few seconds the searchlights went off, one after another in rapid succession. The immediate threat had gone, and their Lancaster flew on to join the main bomber force, which was by now rapidly approaching. Bombing then proceeded as planned.

★ ★ ★

Cliff's second Berlin story is a very unusual one in that it involved a serious dispute, in a crew that had normally worked well together, including the rejection of a decision by the captain – a very serious disciplinary offence. It happened at a time when the crew were in a stressful and challenging situation, with emotions at breaking point.

Their Lancaster had reached the target, having battled its way through the usual barrage of anti-aircraft fire and evaded the night fighters. The bomb aimer took over guidance of the aircraft on the bombing run, and, at the right moment, released the bombs. Around them they were saddened to see other Lancasters, hopelessly damaged, out of control, and plunging to earth. Here and there a few airmen had bailed out and their parachutes were floating nearby.

Their aircraft had flown homeward bound for several miles when the bomb aimer blurted out some startling information:

Bomb aimer: 'Something must be wrong with the release mechanism. Two bombs didn't go. They are still hanging there.'

Pilot: 'OK. Would it be possible to release them manually?'

Bomb aimer: 'Yes, Skip, that can be done.'

Pilot: 'Right. Cliff, will you give me a course to take us back to the target area so we can finish the job?'

Cliff has described his skipper as 'rather a gung-ho type'. He replied:

> Skip, I don't think that's a good idea. Frankly, I think it would be suicidal to go back there when hundreds of other aircraft are just leaving the target area and having to weave and corkscrew to escape from the fighter-bombers. It's hellish back there – a maelstrom.
>
> Of course, we can't return with two bombs that would certainly explode as we touch down. But I can give you a course, on the way back, which will take us to a target we've attacked before, and we can drop the two bombs there.

Pilot: 'Navigator, I've given you my orders. Give me a course back to the target.'

At this point, there was a chorus of protests from the rest of the crew. They made it clear that they were strongly against the notion of returning to the target and backed Cliff's proposal. The captain became very angry.

Pilot: 'Navigator, I've given you my orders. Do you want to be court-martialled for disobeying the orders of your captain?'

There were further protests from the crew and Cliff did not respond. The Lancaster continued on the same course with a silent and rather poisonous atmosphere prevailing.

All that had occurred when nerves were stretched and with emotions running high, but by the time the Lancaster had reached the coast, there had been time for a cooler, more reflective atmosphere to develop. Everyone had calmed down. The crew had achieved a great deal by working together on a number of operations and there was much mutual respect among them. It was the pilot who finally broke the silence: 'Cliff, can you give me a course for home at a nice low altitude, say, 2,000ft, so we can all relax, put everything that's been said behind us, and have a smoke.'

And that's what they did.

15

A LANCASTER GUIDED BY THE STARS

And all I ask is a tall ship,
And a star to steer her by.

John Masefield

The stars provided a reliable navigation aid, and we were completely reliant on them as we prepared for the war against Japan.

Heavenly bodies have been used by sailors for thousands of years. The Vikings, for example, used both the sun and the pole star (Polaris) to sail a line of latitude on their voyages to North America.

In the eighteenth and early nineteenth centuries, Cook, Bligh, Van Couver, and many other sailors achieved great feats of navigation using the stars.

But those sea navigators, looking heavenwards from their vessels, would have often found the sky blanketed with cloud with no stars (or sun or moon) to be seen, and though sextants were invented in 1757, they were at that time relatively crude.

We were much luckier. Flying above 20,000ft, the sky is usually almost clear, with only perhaps delicate ice crystals, which look like wisps of silk (cirrus). Such clouds, along with cirrostratus or cirrocumulus, which also consist of ice crystals, did not significantly restrict my view of the heavens.

The sextant I used, too, had little in common with those used in the eighteenth century, a particularly good feature being the fact that a squeeze of its trigger took fifty rapid 'shots' of a particular star (the one identified and captured in the bubble of the sextant), and then showed the average altitude in a window.

I was so enthusiastic about studying the night sky that when we were not required to fly I often got up in the middle of the night, usually accompanied by our bomb aimer, Jack (at times, a second or assistant navigator), to study stars and constellations. In order to build up a comprehensive knowledge of the night sky, one needs to identify each star in a constellation, and then identify link stars between constellations, until the whole vast panorama of heavenly bodies becomes familiar.

Astronavigation became for me by far the most interesting and absorbing mode of fixing position. It could never be precise, but it was reasonably accurate and I was never unsure of the position of our Lancaster on the longest flights.

Of all the millions of stars in the galaxy, we used only twenty, well spaced around the Northern Hemisphere (today there are fifty-seven navigational stars whose co-ordinates are tabulated in almanacs).

A planisphere, to reveal a picture of the night sky at any particular time and date, was indispensable, especially for flight planning. The one I used was designed by Sir Francis Chichester, who first won fame as an aviator and air navigator well before the Second World War and then, after the war, achieved the great distinction of becoming the first person to sail solo round the world. He thereby became globally recognised as being both a great sailor and an outstandingly skilled air navigator. Whether in the air or at sea, Chichester made good use of the stars.

The planisphere is a simple device, with one disc rotated on a larger one, the two having common centres. The time on the edge of one has to be placed precisely in line with the date on the other. Then, a window reveals the appearance of the night sky in the Northern Hemisphere at that precise time and date.

Using the planisphere, I could decide, well before take-off, which stars, of those visible at that time, I might choose to 'shoot' during various stages of our flight. Much depended on the time of year, because the impressive Orion constellation, for instance, with such magnificent stars as Betelgeuse and Rigel, is visible only during the winter months, while Sirius, the brightest star in the heavens, is nearer to the celestial horizon, and visible for an even shorter time.

To obtain a fix, I would stand up in our noisy, vibrating aircraft, look through the astrodome and scan the night sky to identify my chosen star. Often I would shift my focus from the Plough and Square of Pegasus constellations – always visible in the Northern Hemisphere – towards the star I had in mind. Then I would raise my sextant, fix that star in the bubble and hold it steady while I squeezed the trigger. It wasn't easy to do that in a shuddering aircraft, especially in turbulent conditions. The fifty automatic 'shots' that followed were to allow for vibration and there was plenty of that. At the same time as reading the star's altitude in the window of the sextant, I would take the time to the nearest second, making any adjustment necessary, if my Omega watch was known to be a few seconds fast or slow. Then I would consult the air navigation tables with three pieces of information in mind: the name of the star, its altitude and the time to the nearest second.

The end result was that I could draw a position line on my Mercator chart. Somewhere along that line we had been flying when the shot was taken.

Using the same system as with other aids, I would 'shoot' two more stars, to obtain three position lines altogether, and transfer the first two to the same time as the third one, i.e. to where they would all be if all the 'shots' had been taken at the same time.

As the lines hardly ever intersected completely, but made a little triangle, I would take the centre of that triangle, as our position.

That may all sound a tedious process but it actually worked very well. I couldn't get fixes as often as with radar, but that didn't seem to matter. The courses I was able to give our skipper kept the Lancaster pretty well on track. The stars are always there and they never let you down.

We carried out long flights throughout May, June and early August 1945, by which time I think we must have been regarded as a very highly trained crew, fully ready for any challenges we might meet in the war against Japan. We felt we were ready to be sent to the island of Okinawa.

But it didn't happen. The war in the Pacific ended dramatically, following the dropping of atom bombs on Hiroshima and Nagasaki.

★ ★ ★

Below is a basic explanation of the nature of astronavigation. I believe a broad understanding of how and why astronavigation works enhances interest in it appreciably. It is a branch of applied astronomy and is a fascinating intellectual challenge.

Every heavenly body – stars, sun, moon and planets – is at any one time directly above a point on the Earth's surface. That point is known as its geographical position (GP), and, of course, it moves according to date and time. The measured angle – or altitude – between the celestial body and the horizontal (determined by the sextant shot) is directly related to the distance between the celestial body's GP and the observer. One might imagine a huge circle, sometimes called 'a circle of equal altitude' that is centred on the GP. The observer, or aircraft, is somewhere on that circle.

The navigator's position line is, in fact, a short segment of the very large circle of equal altitude. It doesn't matter that the segment (a curve) is drawn as a straight line on a chart, because that involves a negligible inaccuracy.

IS ASTRONAVIGATION SIMPLY OF HISTORICAL INTEREST?

Many people believe that astronavigation, in the age of satellite navigation, has had its day. Not at all. There is a new, and rapidly growing interest in the subject. In many countries, it is included in the curricula of nautical schools and colleges. Senior crews of most of our large cruise ships are required to develop some expertise in it, in case other (mechanical or satellite) systems fail. The stars are always there and clearly visible.

A few years ago I heard this amusing sextant story from the captain of RMS *Queen Mary 2*, in mid Atlantic, on the way to New York.

A captain he knew had two rules that were virtually laws on board his ship. One was a smoking ban, and the other a requirement that every senior officer should practise using a sextant on a regular basis.

One officer, on duty in the middle of the night, did his duty with a sextant, and then, assuming that the captain was still asleep, dared to smoke a cigarette. One hand held the sextant; the other, the banned cigarette. Suddenly he heard the unmistakable sound of the captain's feet on deck. The captain had woken up early and was approaching. Without a moment's hesitation, the officer threw overboard what he was holding in one hand. But he was in too great a hurry, and it was the wrong hand. He intended to throw the cigarette overboard, but instead threw the sextant!

Avro Lancaster B I PA474 (Battle of Britain Memorial Flight). (Kogo via WikimediaCommons, GNU Free Documentation License, Version 1.2)

★ ★ ★

In October 2015, we learned that the US Navy is going to train all new recruits in astronavigation. Why? Because of rising concern that computers may malfunction. Computers may also be hacked, and cyber terrorists may block GPS. Therefore, although, since 1995 GPS has been able to pinpoint a position to within a few feet, whereas astro-navigation can do so to a mere 1.5 miles, it's a question of backup, and there is no other system as reliable as the stars. Navigators who rely solely on electronic navigation systems could be in great difficulty at some future date.

Captain Timothy Tisch of the US Merchant Marine Academy, explained it in a nutshell:

> Knowledge of celestial navigation, in the GPS era, provides a solid backup. It is good professional practice to use one navigational system to verify the accuracy of another.

Absolutely.

16

WHY ATTACK AT NIGHT?

From the time our crew took over a Wellington, we always flew at night, including all our flying in a Lancaster when we were preparing for the war in the Pacific. It was clearly the intention of the Air Ministry that Japan would not be attacked during daylight hours.

This intention followed the European experience, when night bombing predominated, mainly as a result of the unacceptably high losses experienced during the earlier years of the war, with daytime bombing by Blenheims, Whitleys, Hampdens, Wellingtons and Battles. Towards the end of that first year, on a single operation involving thirty-six bombers, twenty-one failed to return.

It was never the intention of Bomber Command before the war that night bombing would become the norm. The strongly held belief was that, since bombers would be well armed and have machine guns manned by specialist gunners, they would be able to keep at bay, and even destroy, attacking fighter planes. Thus the Wellington was equipped with two machine guns in its forward turret and two in the rear turret. However, that meant that it had no answer to an attack from the side, though some later models had two guns mounted in beam positions. It was thought also that when several Wellingtons were flying in formation, hostile fighter aircraft could be fired on from several angles.

An attack by day would clearly have many advantages over night operations. Map reading would usually be possible and targets would be more easily identified. If the weather were poor – fog or 10/10ths cloud – it would pose even greater problems at night.

The bomber, it was believed, would always get through. This was fallacious thinking, to which also the Luftwaffe was prone, as exemplified during the Battle of Britain. Similarly, the USAAF carried out daytime raids with Flying Fortresses soon after it entered the war, resulting in very heavy losses, in spite of its heavy armaments and the practice of formation flying.

Fighters, which are fast and highly manoeuvrable, are designed to attack and destroy heavier and slower aircraft. Rear gunners of bombers might, and often did, fend off attacking fighters, and sometimes destroy them, but the overall advantage was always with the fighter.

If a formation of bombers were given an escort of fighters, then of course, the situation could be radically different. However, this was rarely possible because of the relatively short range of fighters. For enemy fighters on their home ground the fuel factor was much less significant.

Lessons had to be learnt, and they were learnt, though there was some stubborn clinging to outdated concepts.

On 3 December 1939, it was a very hard lesson, a grim experience. It involved three squadrons of Wellingtons, the best available aircraft, that set out to attack German ships in the Heligoland Bight. German radar identified them early, well before they reached their target, and Luftwaffe fighters were ready for them.

Of the twenty-two Wellingtons, ten were shot down and two others crashed into the sea. Of the other ten, three were so badly damaged that even though they managed to limp back to base, they had to be written off. Therefore only seven survived intact and were available for another operation. Obviously, a loss on this scale, of men and machines, was quite unacceptable.

This experience clearly exposed the limitation that the Wellington's machine guns protected the aircraft only from front and rear, with no defence against attacks from the beam and above.

However, other day raids took place. On 18 December, in the same year, there was an attack on the Schillig Roads and Wilhelmshaven. On that occasion, twelve aircraft were destroyed by fighters and three were badly damaged.

Night bombing meant that navigation problems were greater than they would have been by day. The weather was often worse at night. Especially in foul weather, aircraft sometimes lost their way either outward or homeward bound. If and when they got back on track, they often discovered during their return that their fuel level was dangerously low, yet they often had to join a queue to land.

It was normally colder at night, so there was more chance of icing problems (see Chapter 6). Icing on wings, and iced up engines or instruments might occur, while 10/10ths cloud or fog presented problems at all times, but at night was much worse.

It was more difficult for navigators or other crew members to identify some key features in the blackness of the night, and for bomb aimers to aim with relative precision at a target.

Aircraft attacking at night were brightly illuminated in the sky by the coning of searchlights, focusing on them ready for a barrage of anti-aircraft fire, with night fighters ready to deliver a final blow.

Bombing attacks, whether by day or night, often led to heavy losses, though the night losses were not usually as heavy as the day ones.

★ ★ ★

Derek Waterman DFC, a pilot with 96 and later 158 Squadrons, and the first secretary of our ACA branch, describes attacking a target in the highly defended industrial Ruhr at night.

On his arrival in the target area his crew were confronted with a sky filled black bursts. There were anti-aircraft shells bursting all around them. On the bombing run, his bomb aimer, Reg, requested that the bomb doors be opened. Derek describes the operation:

'OK, Reg. Bomb doors open.'

No longer were voices calm and steady. We now shouted. We were tense and tempers were short. 'Five degrees starboard!' yelled Reg. 'OK, keep her there – left, left, bit more, left, left, steady, steady.'

It was now a struggle to keep the aircraft on an even keel. The slipstream from those in front tossed us about and made it difficult to fly straight and level. The flak was intense and I could smell cordite. Its unpleasantly pungent smell meant that the bursts were dangerously close. There was a loud bang; then a noise like hail rattling on a corrugated iron roof. We had been hit, but how badly I did not know. The aircraft still responded to the controls, and that was the main thing. Reg spoke again: 'Bombs gone – keep her steady, we want a good photo.'

I had to fly as straight and as level as possible to get a good photo.

The operation completed, Derek turned the aircraft on to the course for the first leg of the homeward journey. But they were by no means out of danger.

'I saw a Halifax receive a direct hit from a shell, and burst into a thousand pieces. No parachutes emerged.'

Soon they were on their way home.

'I would see June tonight – perhaps go to the pictures. It seemed such a contrast to the hell we had just left in our wake.'

That last comment well illustrates the fact that airmen on operations had to manage, on almost a daily basis, the eerily challenging adaptation, from living a fairly normal life during the day, to enduring the most dangerous confrontations of the war, at night.

17

THE BRAVERY OF AIR GUNNERS

Elsewhere I have emphasised the particular vulnerability of gunners, especially rear gunners. Their expectation of life might be not much other than a few weeks. They were the main targets of night fighters, which sought to eliminate the rear gunner before attacking more vulnerable parts of the aircraft. Some 20,000 gunners died during the Second World War, over a third of total aircrew fatalities. Returning aircraft often contained dead and wounded airmen, and they were often the rear gunners.

Sometimes, the whole of the rear turret was blown off by enemy shells and cannon fire.

The rear turret of a bomber during a night operation was so cramped that it was difficult to move. Many gunners found it impossible to climb into their turrets wearing their flying boots so they threw them in before climbing in themselves. They could hardly move their legs and might have to endure such a cramped position for up to ten hours.

The temperature in the rear turret was often freezing (sometimes as low as minus 40 degrees Celsius), as the aircraft's heating did not reach that far, and the gunner's electronically heated suits were sometimes almost useless. Rear gunners were often very cold and frostbite was not uncommon.

Whereas most other crew members were close together near the front of the aircraft, and had the benefit of close companionship, the gunners were relatively isolated. The mid-upper gunner was further back in the aircraft, suspended on a canvas sling sheet, with his head in a flexi-glass dome. The rear gunner was even more isolated at the tail of the aircraft.

The rear gunner could never relax. Throughout the flight over enemy territory, and sometimes when homeward bound, he constantly rotated his turret to scan the air for fighters. He had the responsibility for spotting any attacks from the rear and for sometimes calling on the pilot to begin an evasive manoeuvre, such as 'Corkscrew to starboard, Skip!' or 'Dive, Skip!'.

Many, perhaps most, air gunners were 19 or 20, but some were even younger and a few considerably older.

The youngest one was probably a Canadian, Flight Sergeant Edward James Wright, air gunner of a Lancaster of 428 Squadron. Only 16 years of age, he was killed on 30 April 1945, shortly before the end of the war.

The oldest rear gunner was William Wedgewood Benn DSO DFC, father of the politician Tony Benn. A pilot in the Royal Flying Corps, during the First World War, he joined up as a pilot officer in 1940, rose to become an air commodore, retrained as an air gunner and in that capacity flew on several operations aged 67!

Below are three examples of the outstanding bravery of rear gunners.

★ ★ ★

In the early years of the war John Hannah, a wireless operator/air gunner, was flying in a Hampden bomber over Antwerp, having successfully bombed some barge concentrations when the aircraft received a direct hit. Suddenly there were flames everywhere: 'The whole of the bomb compartment, with the draught coming through the large holes blown out … turned into a sort of blow torch.'

The aluminium floor of the air gunner's turret melted in the heat: 'This molten metal was blown backwards and plated in great smears on the rear bulkheads.'

The air gunner beat out the flames with his logbook. The aircraft reached base with 'a hole in the fuselage big enough for a man to crawl through'.

The rear gunner's turret and half the interior of the fuselage were charred ruins. There were holes in the wings and in the petrol tanks.

The wireless operator/air gunner, who was badly burned, received the Victoria Cross. He had saved the lives of the crew and enabled the aircraft to be saved.[1]

★ ★ ★

There was a raid by Wellingtons on Brest, in which 104 Squadron took part, in 1941. One aircraft completed its task and headed for home, mainly in the direction of Cornwall, but was attacked by a Messerschmitt 109. The rear gunner, John Armstrong, was hit by a bullet in the shin. In spite of that, he left his turret to put out a blaze in the fuselage. He then returned, but so did the Messerschmitt. The Perspex of his turret was soon shattered by a stream of bullets, and an oil line was ruptured, the leaking sticky, black fluid covering John. A bullet then hit him in the thigh and there was a new fire in the fuselage. He went to put out that blaze and was helped by the navigator. They managed to extinguish the fire, but John then collapsed.[2]

* * *

For the next Wellington story I am indebted to the *Mail Online*. An article from 18 June 2016 was about Flight Lieutenant Freddie Johnson DFC, a rear gunner, who flew on ninety-two bombing operations – a truly great achievement – in two of which his aircraft was shot down.

Freddie flew in Germany (twenty-five operations), Burma and North Africa.

On one of his early missions, his aircraft was hit 100 times. It was at El Alamein, the famous North African location where Britain's Eighth Army began its famous attack, that Freddie's aircraft crashed in the desert. He survived because of an incredibly lucky event. His turret actually came away from the rest of the aircraft as it crashed. The fuselage then exploded, killing the other four crew members. Freddie then climbed out of the turret. That he was able to do so is astonishing.

Freddie knew that he was behind enemy lines and began a trek across the desert, which ended only when some British soldiers picked him up.

The second crash occurred on the India–Burma border when once again Freddie's aircraft was shot down. Miraculously, on this occasion, all crew members survived.

After the war, he was happy to speak to various groups. To one he remarked how lucky he had been to survive and told the following story:

> On one raid, a shell came straight up between my legs. It took off the top of my turret and also two of my guns … I remember peering out of the gaping hole and watching my guns fall over Paris.

Freddie still bore the scars of war. A leg was injured in one operation and he had pins put in his legs.

He died on 20 April 2013. Some days later he was laid to rest following a funeral, with full military honours, at St Mary's Church, Tadcaster. The man who had flown ninety-two operations had died aged 92.

* * *

I wonder how many similar stories could be told. Numerous outstanding acts of bravery were, no doubt, never recorded. Some had no witnesses. Of course, any member of a crew might be involved in an act of selfless courage but the lonely gunner, often the youngest of their crew, had to be ever watchful, and this poem expresses so well his isolation, his huge responsibility and his vulnerability:

Alone in his transparent shell,
A speck in space,
He sits, poised in his airy kingdom.
At his back the unknown,
Before him the unfolding map
Of his journey.
Guardian of seven lives

Taut with the concentration of survival,
He swings his turret through vigilant arcs,
Eyes straining for the fighters.
Braced for the violence of surprise.

Philip A. Nicholson
(Bomber Command Museum of Canada.
Nanton Lancaster Society)

★ ★ ★

OPERATION MANNA

Here is something quite different, in which an air gunner, Warrant Officer Ron Liversage MBE of our ACA branch (see also Chapter 6) was involved. Following his tour of thirty operations in Lancasters, Ron took part in a humanitarian operation during the last few weeks of the war, when his aircraft dropped food instead of bombs.

Many people in Holland were virtually starving towards the end of hostilities; 20,000 people had already starved to death. 3,156 Lancasters and 145 Mosquitos dropped 7,030 tons of food from a low altitude on to the racecourse at The Hague and elsewhere. The food was seized with relief and joy, and in one field a message was laid out in tulips: 'Thank you boys.'

The Dutch people showed their appreciation for many years after the war. Ron has described how he and others went back to Holland year after year and that there was a special celebration there in 1999, after twenty-five years of annual visits, when he met some of the recipients of the food and danced with a lady of 90.

NOTES

1 *Bomber Command*, 1941, page 69
2 *RAF Bomber Command at War*, page 69

18

THE LANCASTERS OF TIGER FORCE: FACTS AND SPECULATIONS

Who has ever heard of TIGER FORCE? Very few people, I imagine. It was going to attack Japan, following the European war.

Bomber Command, although fully stretched in Europe, was keen to plan the bombing of our enemy in the Pacific. At one time, during 1944, there was a plan for air attacks on it from bases in Burma! The flights would have been very long and the problems considerable, including carrying sufficient fuel for the enormous distances to be covered.

In that connection, it was envisaged that Lancasters might be equipped with 640-gallon tanks in the bomb bays and 580 gallons in each wing tank. There were also tentative plans for saddle tanks to be fitted to the top of Lancasters, after removal of the mid-upper turret, which would involve the loss of a key part of the aircraft's armament.

The USA offered the island of Okinawa, 800 miles from Tokyo, for our base, and was also willing to provide fighter escorts for our bombers, augmenting some Australian fighter planes. The Commonwealth forces would have had to build their own airfields.

Even using Okinawa, there would still be the question of how to provide fuel for such a long flight. Trials indicated that in-flight refuelling could be carried out, and plans for that were well advanced. Perhaps half of the Lancasters might be aerial tankers refuelling the other half, at least until there were sufficient Lincolns – developed from the Lancasters – to replace the latter. The Lancasters would fly in pairs, side by side.

In-flight refuelling would need to take place during daylight hours. This was likely to be difficult and dangerous when there were many aircraft within a limited air space. Frequent attacks by Japanese fighter planes could be anticipated.

Bomber Command did not favour in-flight fuelling, how-ever, and that idea was finally abandoned on 18 April 1945 in favour of using Lincolns, with saddle tanks. The Lincolns would therefore have been deprived of mid upper turrets with their machine guns to ward off attacks from above. The saddle tanks would also have reduced both the speed and the manoeuvrability of the Lincoln to a degree.

The Quebec Conference in September 1944 between Churchill and Roosevelt planned the greater co-ordination of our forces in the Pacific area in order to bring about the end of that war as soon as possible. That's when TIGER FORCE was formally planned. It was to operate from the autumn of 1945.

The final agreement – initial plans were steadily watered down – was that TIGER FORCE would consist of ten squadrons of heavy bombers in two groups, consisting of

Lancasters, Lincolns and Liberators, with fighter escorts. It would be a Commonwealth force.

Every aircraft in it would be painted white on the upper surfaces and black underneath.

Among the many problems, that emerged was the question of manpower. Seasoned airmen who felt they had 'done their bit' in Europe were often anxious to be demobilised when the European war ended rather than become involved in another war. Some airmen, who had been POWs, were hurriedly retrained to fly Lancasters. TIGER FORCE would have probably had too many inexperienced air crews (like ours!). Assembling adequate numbers of ground crew staff, including engineers, could also have been problematical.

Had our crew joined TIGER FORCE in 1945, as planned, I wonder what would have been the most likely outcome? For example, would the air war over Japan have been even more dangerous than it was over Germany, where nearly half our crews perished?

But first, my crew would have been required, with many others, to fly our Lancaster out from Britain to the Pacific island of Okinawa with myself, as navigator, providing our skipper with courses based on the stars. I can think of several problems likely to have occurred on such a marathon flight at that time.

It would, of course, have been flown as a series of legs so that fuelling, maintenance and rest would be available at appropriate points.

We would not have had the wonderful support of our UK ground staff, while the RAF's Far Eastern staff would have been largely unfamiliar with the Lancaster (although some Lancasters had flown in India). RAF stations en route may have been well serviced and equipped, but there would have been a shortage of emergency airfields, and emergencies would surely have occurred.

From the evidence of other crews in the East, we know that most of the available maps would have been inadequate or obsolete. Nor would we have had the benefit of reliable weather forecasts, including forecast wind velocities.

In addition, the absence of alternative modes of navigation could have caused problems. Astronavigation, of course, would be used mainly at night, but during the day we would have had to depend, to a degree, on map reading. The difficulties of doing so in such areas, and at that time, is described by Tom Winup when he was on secret operations, flying eastwards from India (see Chapter 3).

Regarding the prospect of attacking from Okinawa, it can be assumed that the defences of Japan would have been at least as potent as Germany's, in terms of anti-aircraft gunfire and night fighters.

I don't know which Japanese aircraft were adapted as night fighters but she certainly had some formidable fighter planes.

The Mitsubishi A6M Zero, available at the start of the war, was arguably the most advanced fighter anywhere at that time. It was highly manoeuvrable, armed with two 20mm cannons, and had a range of 1,844 miles.

The Kawanishi N1K-J Shiden was perhaps the best Japanese fighter of the whole war. It had a powerful engine, was highly manoeuvrable, had a top speed over 400mph, and was heavily armed, with four 20mm cannon. It had many successes in the latter stages of the war.

The Kyushu J7W Shinden was designed especially to combat the USA's Superfortresses. It was seen as Japan's 'wonder weapon', but only two were ever built. No doubt it would have been mass-produced had the war continued.

In addition to these highly efficient aircraft, we would have been faced with Japanese kamikazi (suicide) pilots who would have simply crashed their aircraft into ours, while her anti-aircraft guns and fighter aircraft would have been deployed in dense concentrations along her coast, much of which might well have been almost impenetrable.

Japan consists mainly of four main islands – Hokkaido, Honshu, Shikoku and Kyushu. It stretches over a wide latitude and many potential targets such as ports, factories, marshalling yards and airfields, would have been a very long way from Okinawa.

At the Yalta Conference in February 1945 Stalin's agreement that two of the USSR bases in the Far East could be used by American B-29 bombers could have been valuable for them, and I understand that some Lancasters might have operated from a Chinese airfield.

As the Japanese coast extends more or less in a north–south direction, our aircraft flying from Okinawa would have needed to fly long distances near the coast and we would undoubtedly have been under attack from both anti-aircraft guns and night fighters for much of the flight.

Then there is the intriguing question of the role of our fighter escorts. Fighters have a relatively short range and would have been able to escort our heavy bombers for only part of the way to targets in, for example Osaka, Nagoya, Yokohama or Tokyo on the island of Honshu, while it is an enormous distance to Sapporo in Hokkaido, which is further north than Vladivostok. Without fighter escort, our bombers, however formidable their armaments, would have been no match for the Japanese fighters.

Probably, bomber aircraft flying from Okinawa would have flown part of the way with a fighter escort during the daytime and the fighters would have then turned back, leaving the bombers to continue towards their target without an escort as night-time approached.

Happily, none of these gloomy thoughts occurred to me or my fellow crew members at the time. Frankly we didn't know enough about the situation into which we would soon find ourselves. We were cheerfully optimistic.

Of course, we didn't need to fly to Okinawa.

On 6 August 1945, the Americans in a B-29 Superfortress called *The Enola Gray* dropped an atom bomb on Hiroshima.

On 9 August, another atom bomb was dropped on Nagasaki.

On 14 August, 752 B-29 bombers attacked seven different targets in Japan, operations that appear to have been superfluous in view of the shattering events earlier.

The following day, the Japanese Emperor, Hirohito, broadcast the surrender of his nation.

The response of Bomber Command to these developments was immediate. Our Lancaster – and all others – was grounded, and we crew members were sent away on indefinite leave.

We didn't realise it at the time but we would never see one another again, which was sad.

AFTERWORD

Many of the incidents and experiences described earlier were weather-related. Ice on wings; frozen radio, engines or altimeter; cumulonimbus clouds; electrical storms; and impenetrable fog: all, whether singly or in combination, presented a threat to aircraft and their crews.

Such problems seem to have been particularly severe during the early years of the war, when crews were flying Battles, Blenheims, Whitleys, Wellingtons and Hampdens (see Appendix). Those aircraft were not always fit for purpose, while the enemy their crews faced was often underestimated by the planners.

Later, heavy bombers such as the Halifax and Stirling were more suited to the tasks set. They were followed by the Lancaster and Mosquito, which were better designed, faster, and equipped with more reliable systems.

Altogether, Britain made enormous strides during the war, with great increases in the number and quality of its aircraft, with the development of sophisticated navigational radar devices such as Gee, H2S and Oboe and with improvements in armaments.

But so, too, did the Germans. For instance, between January and August 1943, the strength of the Luftwaffe actually doubled, with a great expansion in the number of night fighters, whose attacks became increasingly effective. For example, of the 123 bombers lost during three raids on Berlin in 1943, about eighty fell to night fighters. Germany's technology developed in parallel with the growing Luftwaffe, with radar playing an increasing role in both defence and attack. From 1942 it was used to guide searchlights and anti-aircraft fire that operated together to destroy our aircraft, then suddenly brought their activities to an end to allow night fighters to take over for the kill.

★ ★ ★

Throughout the war, the outcome of the air struggles over Germany depended on which side had command of the air at any time. Bomber Command achieved that when its bombers, in daylight, with Spitfires flying alongside, attacked continental coastal areas in 1941–42, but the limited range of fighter planes was a restricting factor. Another example was when the Mustang was fitted with a supercharger and extra fuel tanks. It was then able to escort B-17 bombers.

For the most part, however, command of the air was not possible during a normal bombing operation when highly manoeuvrable, heavily armed night fighters were deployed in strength. The Luftwaffe possessed about 1,000 night fighters by 1943.

★ ★ ★

Navigators were at one time called observers. Beyond the range of radar, and radio contact, accurate map reading could be crucially important. Yet sometimes there was

10/10ths cloud for long periods, obscuring all landmarks – coastlines, towns, rivers and other significant features.

Many reports from both pilots and navigators make it clear that aircraft often lost their way, sometimes on the outward flight of an operation, sometimes on the flight home.

Perhaps the most disastrous example of the effects of atrocious weather is in the well-researched book *Black Night for Bomber Command* by Richard Knott.

On 16 December 1943 328 airmen died, perhaps nearly half of whom were victims of the weather, not enemy action. The target was Berlin, which involved a flight from bases in eastern England of about seven hours and a round trip of 1,150 miles. There were 500 aircraft involved. The weather was awful all the way and outside radar range the navigational difficulties increased.

Homeward bound, the crews were unable to see anything below the aircraft. Many navigators were at times unsure of their position and were forced to depend on their flight plan with its out-of-date wind velocity forecasts. Consequently, many aircraft returned along routes well away from planned ones so that extra fuel was used, leaving barely enough for the homeward flight.

Some crews, when close to their base, faced perilous conditions on their descent. It was impossible to identify any landmarks through the murky fog and, as they were running out of fuel, time was of the essence. Dipping down through the fog to try to identify something involved a great danger of collisions, not only with other aircraft but potentially with transmission cables, hangars, trees and hills.

★ ★ ★

In addition to the problems discussed above, there was one other factor that could be significant. While all bomber crews had a very thorough training, what they often lacked was experience. Their average age was 22, but a large number were only 18 or 19.

The losses on operations were sometimes very heavy, the heaviest of all being when there was an attack on Nuremberg on 30 March 1944, when ninety-five (of 796) bombers were destroyed, mainly by night fighters, and ten others were so badly damaged that they had to be written off after landing. Therefore, the total loss of aircraft was 105 (11 per cent) and 535 lives were lost.

It was clearly difficult for Bomber Command to maintain a series of attacks with up to 1,000 bombers, in view of the heavy losses frequently suffered. Consequently, young crews were often allocated to a squadron as soon as their training was over, and quickly sent on operations. Also, crews still with Training Command sometimes took part in operations. The Thousand Bomber operations always involved the use of novice crews. There can be no doubt that partly because of this, accidents and errors, especially in piloting or navigation, were often as high as they were. It was found that a crew's first five operations were the most dangerous ones and many novice crews died on their first operation.

I write as a member of one of the novice crews but it just so happened that we were not called upon to participate in such operations, perhaps because we were already ear-marked for the war in the Pacific. During the European war we were used only for a few diversionary or spoof raids that helped sometimes to fool the Germans as to where the main attack was to come from. Or we might be engaged in dropping foil to upset the enemy's radar.

That rather marginal involvement in the European thea-tre greatly enhanced my admiration of all those airmen who flew one operation after another, and who learnt, day after day, of yet more friends who had sadly 'gone for a Burton' the previous night. Yet RAF aircrews, seasoned and otherwise, maintained, to a considerable degree, their high morale and good humour throughout the war. *Esprit de corps* really meant something.

* * *

There are several references in the text to the radar aids: Gee, H2S and Oboe.

Gee was a receiver in the aircraft for two synchronised pulses transmitted from the UK. The time delay between the two pulses enabled the Gee receiver to calculate the aircraft's position (an aerial was mounted on top of the fuselage ahead of the mid-upper turret). The range of Gee, however, was limited to about 400 miles.

H2S provided a useful map-reading facility, with the illuminated outline of towns, coastline and rivers showing up clearly, whatever the weather, but German night fighters were eventually able to home in on it.

Oboe was a very accurate navigation system with a receiver/transmitter for two radar stations transmitting from widely separate locations in Southern England. As with Gee and H2S, however, its range was limited.

Fitted to the wonderfully fast and highly manoeuvrable Mosquito, and flown by a Pathfinder crew to mark a target, it could be extremely effective, as on the attack on the Krupp works at Essen, and other industrial targets in the Ruhr, especially from March to July 1943.

In my Lancaster, both Gee and H2S consoles, in the form of two rather ancient-looking TV sets, were near my work table, and when I used them, in the early years of 1945, they made possible very accurate navigation.

★ ★ ★

Finally, I must relate one of the most heart-warming stories of wartime operations – and it had a happy ending.

Sergeant Norman Jackson VC (1919–94) a flight engineer in a Lancaster of 106 Squadron, had, by April 1944, completed thirty operations and was due to return home. However, he decided to join his regular crew for a last operation.

On 26 April they took part in the bombing of the ball-bearing factory at Schweinfurt. Turning for home, their aircraft was attacked by both anti-aircraft fire and a night fighter. Norman was wounded by shell splinters and the right wing of the aircraft was soon ablaze dangerously close to the fuel tank.

In spite of his injuries, Norman volunteered to put out the fire. He strapped on a parachute, grabbed a fire extinguisher and climbed on to the flaming wing. The aircraft was flying at 20,000ft, where there was little oxygen, so he could easily have lost consciousness, quite apart from being at the mercy of the roaring, gale-like slipstream, which threatened to sweep him away.

After a struggle, Norman managed to put out the fire but then the night fighter returned to the attack and two of its bullets hit him in the leg. He was now badly burned, wounded and exhausted. He was finally blown off the wing, plummeting to the earth, his parachute – which had opened – alight and smouldering.

Amazingly he reached the earth safely but had a broken ankle to add to his extensive burns and wounds. He was soon captured and paraded through the streets in spite of his injuries.

Norman then spent ten months in a German hospital, followed by some time in a POW camp. He made two attempts to escape, the second of which was successful. He later learned that four of his crew survived and two did not.

Back in England, Norman received the VC from King George VI at the same time as Wing Commander (later Group Captain) Cheshire, who had completed 102 operations and nearly four tours. The latter suggested to the King that Norman was the greater hero and should receive his award first, but the King had to follow protocol and deal first with the senior officer.

Norman and his wife Alma had six children. His eyes and hands never properly healed.

APPENDIX

RAF MEDIUM AND LIGHT BOMBERS AT THE START OF THE SECOND WORLD WAR

The aircraft that are mentioned in this book as being used in the early years of the war are the Wellington, Blenheim, Battle, Whitley, Hampden and Swordfish. The Wellington has been described at the beginning of Chapter 5. Below are brief descriptions of the others.

Each of those aircraft had some successes, but although most were by no means old – in 1935, the Wellingtons, Whitleys and Hampdens were all new – they were all obsolete to a degree when Britain declared war on 3 September 1939, such had been the rapid pace of technology development during the 1930s.

Bristol Blenheim

The Blenheim, powered by two radial engines and with a crew of three, was in service with the RAF from 1937. With a maximum speed of 266mph, it was relatively fast and was

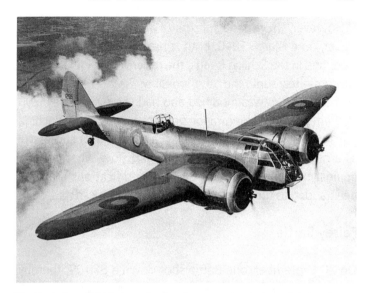

The Blenheim, a light twin-engine bomber, was extensively used during the first two years of the Second World War. It was one of the first British aircraft with retractable landing gear, flaps, a powered gun turret and variable pitch propellers. (Canadian Forces/Wikimedia Commons)

regarded as potentially a very effective medium bomber. However, it was armed with only a Vickers machine gun in the rear turret and another forward-firing Browning machine gun outboard of the port engine, and was no match for Luftwaffe fighters.

For example, twelve Blenheims attacked German tanks and troops near Gembleux on 17 May 1940, ten of which were shot down by fighters while another was destroyed by anti-aircraft fire. Two of the crews that bailed out eventually returned to England and several wounded airmen were picked up.

On 13 August 1940 eleven Blenheims attacked a Luftwaffe airfield in Denmark and all were shot down. These were terrible losses of which the British public was unaware at the time.

However, they made successful attacks on two U-boats earlier, on 4 March 1940. Both submarines were on the surface, one in the Schillig Roads, the other off Heligoland. One was definitely sunk; the other possibly.

The Blenheim was modified and had some successes, 200 of them becoming long-range fighter versions, with machine guns under the fuselage, and it was reasonably successful as a night fighter. However, it was too slow when ranged against the Luftwaffe's Bf 109, the modifications that had been added to the aircraft's weight having reduced its speed.

Fairey Battle

On 20 September, one Battle shot down a Bf 109, thereby registering the first kill of the war, but thereafter its successes were rare.

The Battle was a light bomber with a single Rolls-Royce engine, a three-man crew (pilot, navigator, gunner) and

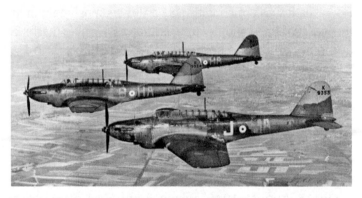

The Fairey Battle, a twin-engine light bomber with a three-man crew, did not live up to expectations. Used in the early years of the war, its losses were often over 50 per cent. Equipped with only two machine guns, with a very limited range and a fairly slow speed, it was withdrawn by the end of 1940. (John Gerrard collection)

carried 1,000lb of bombs. It looked like an oversized fighter, but with a top speed of 257mph it was almost 100mph slower than the Luftwaffe's Bf 109. It had one machine gun in the rear cockpit and another forward-firing one in the starboard wing.

On 10 May 1940 there were two sorties. In the first, three of eight were shot down; in the second, ten of twenty-four were lost. In one attack on 11 May, against a German column by eight aircraft, only one survived.

Three days later, six Battles attacked bridges across the Albert Canal. Five were shot down and the sixth crashed after the crew had bailed out over our lines. One end of a bridge had been demolished. Two VCs were awarded to crews of the leading aircraft.

Also that May, sixty-seven Battles attacked bridges being crossed by Germans across the River Meuse. Two pontoon bridges were destroyed and two permanent bridges received direct hits, but delays to the German advance were only temporary.

Only thirty-two Battles returned. The crew of six of the crashed aircraft, who had bailed out, gradually managed to return to their bases in France.

Altogether by May 1940, 50 per cent of all Battles sent on sorties had been lost. These were terrible losses.

The Battle was not used for bombing operations after October 1940.

Armstrong Whitworth Whitley

The Whitley was always intended for night bombing. Powered with two Rolls-Royce Merlin engines, and with a crew of five, it had a strange appearance as the wings were set at a high angle of incidence to assist take-off and landing. That caused it to fly with a nose-down attitude, which

An excellent photograph looking down on the Whitley. (Originally featured in *The Aeroplane*, and reproduced here with kind permission of Key Publishing Ltd)

caused considerable drag and slowed it down significantly, so there was apparently a serious fault in its design.

Another disadvantage it shared with many other aircraft such as the Wellington is that it could not maintain height with only one engine, so if one were put out of action, it could be doomed.

It was retired from front-line service in April 1942, but took part in the Thousand Bomber Raid on Cologne on 30 May that year.

Handley Page Hampden

The Hampden was a twin-engine medium bomber with a crew of four (pilot, navigator/bomb aimer, radio operator, rear gunner), which was a little newer than the others available. It carried 4,000lb of bombs and had one fixed machine gun in the nose and one or two in each of the rear dorsal and ventral positions. Its armaments were inadequate, however, and it did not stand much chance against Luftwaffe fighters.

It was very narrow and cramped, which caused it to be known as 'the flying suitcase'.

On 29 September 1939, Hampdens patrolling Heligoland Bight in formations of five and six attacked two U-boats, and were themselves attacked by German fighters. Of the group of six, none returned. Two of the fighters were shot down.

Almost half of the 714 Hampdens that were built were lost on operations, causing 1,077 deaths with another 739 airmen missing. It was withdrawn from front-line bombing in 1942.

Fairey Swordfish

Although this book is mainly concerned with the crews of Bomber Command, Chapter 6 includes the experience of Ken Dixon of the Fleet Air Arm and a member of our ACA branch.

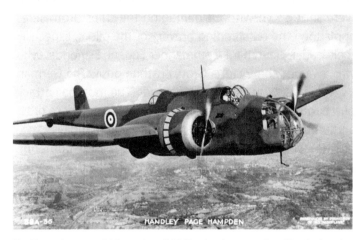

The Hampden was widely used until 1942 when it was replaced by the heavier, four-engine Lancasters and Halifaxes. However, it was involved in the first raid on Berlin and the first Thousand Bomber Raid on Cologne. (Originally featured in *The Aeroplane*, and reproduced here with kind permission of Key Publishing Ltd)

Ken's Swordfish, with others, guarded a convoy taking essential war supplies to Russia. They headed for the port of Murmansk, in the Arctic Circle, an extremely hazardous operation that was successfully completed in spite of Junkers 88 dive-bombers and U-boats, and having to fly in polar conditions (see page 68).

The Swordfish really was a remarkable little aircraft. A biplane, resembling perhaps those of the First World War, it was certainly outdated by 1939, yet it remained in front-line service throughout the European war.

It had some outstanding successes, including sinking or damaging two battleships. On anti-submarine duties with convoys, it carried aerial torpedoes (as in the picture opposite), and it could also act as a dive-bomber. However, its speed was too slow and it suffered serious losses against well-defended targets.

An attack on the battleships *Scharnhorst* and *Gneisnau*, in February 1942, was both heroic and tragic. All six Swordfish were shot down without damaging the ships. Both sides applauded the outstanding bravery of the pilots, especially their leader, Lieutenant Commander Eugene Esmonde, who was awarded the Victoria Cross posthumously. The German Vice Admiral Otto Ciliax commented: 'The mothball attack of a handful of ancient planes, piloted by men whose bravery surpasses any other action by either side that day ...'

The Swordfish was more successful in anti-submarine attacks with depth charges or with eight rockets.

Someone referred to the Swordfish as 'an unsung hero of the Allied cause against Axis naval forces'.

* * *

A biplane, with its fixed 'pram wheels' undercarriage, the Swordfish certainly suggested the First World War rather than the Second. However, with an underslung torpedo, as here, rockets and depth charges, it could be effective against submarines. (SDASM archives)

In the period 1939 to 1941 Britain's aircraft, apart from the Spitfire and Hurricane, were simply not adequate for the tasks assigned to them but we had to use the only aircraft we possessed at that time. However, in all these aircraft there were crews who fought bravely. Many examples are in the main text but here is another one …

Flight Lieutenant Rod Learoyd led an attack by Hampdens on the Dortmund–Ems canal on 12 August 1940. He flew over the target as low as 150ft for maximum accuracy, and inevitably his aircraft became the main focus of search-lights and anti-aircraft fire. The aircraft was badly damaged, especially the hydraulic system, the wing flaps and the undercarriage. Nevertheless, Learoyd pressed on with his attack, bombed the target, and flew the aircraft back to base. However, he decided that it would be dangerous to land with his severely damaged Hampden in the dark, so he circled round until first light, when he made a safe landing. He was awarded the Victoria Cross for his bravery and for saving the aircraft and the lives of all his crew.

BIBLIOGRAPHY

Air Ministry *Bomber Command Handbook* (London: HMSO, 1941)

Barker, Ralph *The RAF at War* (London: Time-Life Books, 1981)

Bowman, Martin W. *Flying into the Flames of Hell* (Barnsley: Pen and Sword, 2006)

Fielder, Mark, Executive Producer, BBC Battlefield Series, *The Air War and British Bomber Crews in World War Two*

Hastings, Max *Bomber Command* (London: Michael Joseph, 1979)

Jackson, Robert *Before the Storm: The Story of Bomber Command 1939–1942* (London: Cassell, 2000)

Knott, Richard *Black Night for Bomber Command* (Barnsley: Pen and Sword, 2007)

Liddell Hart, B.H. *A History of the Second World War* (London: Cassell, 1970)

Matthews, Rupert *RAF Bomber Command at War* (Wiltshire: Robert Hale Ltd, 2009)

Middlebrook, Martin The Berlin Raids (London: Viking, 1988)

Radell, Rick and Vines, Mike *Lancaster: A Bombing Legend* (Oxford: Osprey Publishing, 1993)

Read, Simon *The Killing Skies: RAF Bomber Command at War* (Stroud: Spellmount, 2006)

Richards, Denis *The Hardest Victory: RAF Bomber Command in the Second World War* (London: Penguin, 2007)

Smith, Ron *Rear Gunner Pathfinders* (Manchester: Crécy Publishing, 1997)

Sweetman, John *Bomber Command*, (London: Little, Brown Book Group, 2004)

Tedder, Lord *With Prejudice, The War Memoirs of Marshal of the Royal Air Force Lord Tedder G.C.B.* (London: Cassell, 1966)

Thorburn, Gordon *Bombers First and Last* (London: Robson Books, 2006)

Tweddle, Paul *Into the Night Sky, RAF Middleton St George. A Bomber Command at War* (Stroud: Sutton Publishers, 2007)

Webster, C. and Frankland, N. *The Strategic Air Offensive Against Germany 1935–45* (London: Official History, HMSO, 1961)

Wilson, Kevin *Men of Air* (London: Weidenfeld and Nicolson, 2007)